READING
IN THE CONTENT AREAS

Advanced

READING IN THE CONTENT AREAS

An Interactive Approach
for
International
Students

PATRICIA A. RICHARD-AMATO

Longman

Reading in the Content Areas: An Interactive Approach for International Students

Longman, 95 Church Street, White Plains, N.Y. 10601

Associated companies:
Longman Group Ltd., London
Longman Cheshire Pty., Melbourne
Longman Paul Pty., Auckland
Copp Clark Pitman, Toronto

Distributed in the United Kingdom by Longman Group
Ltd., Longman House, Burnt Mill, Harlow, Essex CM20
2JE, England, and by associated companies, branches,
and representatives throughout the world.

Executive editor: Joanne Dresner
Development editor: Penny Laporte
Production editor: Linda Carbone
Text design: Design Five, NYC
Cover design: Joseph DePinho
Photo Research: Elizabeth Barker, Polli Heyden

Credits can be found on pages 103–104.

Library of Congress Cataloging-in-Publication Data

Reading in the content areas: an interactive approach / [edited by]
    Patricia A. Richard-Amato.
        p.   cm.
    Contents: A sociological perspective/Donald A. Hobbs and Stuart J. Blank — Creativity/Duane and Sarah
Preble — The famous deaf composer: Ludwig van Beethoven/Roger Kamien — The impact of computers
on people/Donald H. Sanders — Survival in the wild: the predator and the prey/Cecie Starr and Ralph
Taggart —Immigrants to the United States during the nineteenth century/Robert Divine . . . [et al.] — An
occurrence at Owl Creek bridge/Ambrose Bierce — Economic Resources, Power, and Prestige/Carol R.
Ember and Melvin Ember — Numeral systems/Howard Eves — Research foundations/Philip G. Zimbardo.
    ISBN 0–8013–0247–1
    1. Readers (Adult) 2. Interdisciplinary approach in education. 3. English language—Textbooks for foreign
speakers.
    I. Richard-Amato, Patricia A.
PE1126.A4R43   1990
428.6'4—dc20

                                                                                                89–27555
                                                                                                CIP

BCDEFGHIJ-HC-99 98 97 96 95 94 93 92 91 90

For my mother
Myrtle Forsythe Abbott

CONTENTS

TO THE TEACHER

What Is an Interactive Approach to Skills Development?

An interactive approach to skills development is one that requires an interplay between reader and text and between reader and others in the classroom and its surroundings. The skills (in this case, those related to reading) are taught through a *focus on the reader.* The reader's prior knowledge, culture, valuing systems, relationships, dreams, and goals are explored in relation to the content.

The book treats skills not as isolated elements to master but as strategies to comprehend and extend the meaning of the readings.

What Skill Areas Are Included?

Some of the skill areas included in the book are comprehending intended meaning; internalizing knowledge; applying knowledge; synthesizing experience; relating to cultural background; predicting and/or anticipating content; making inferences; reading critically; taking advantage of the knowledge of others; exploring organizational patterns; finding support for conclusions; distinguishing fact from opinion; discovering themes, irony, metaphor, and other literary devices; interpreting graphs, charts, and tables; and creating outlines and clustering devices to facilitate long-term memory.

For Whom Is the Book Intended?

The book is intended for older adolescent and adult students who are operating at advanced levels in English as a second or foreign language. Most are preparing for study in various fields at English-speaking colleges or universities.

What Kinds of Readings Are Presented?

The readings are all taken from textbooks in current use in colleges and universities on English-speaking campuses. They come from ten different content areas: sociology, art, music, business, natural science, history, literature, anthropology, mathematics, and psychology.

The selections included were chosen not only because of their content but because of their general appeal to students. Although the readings are nontechnical, they are, nevertheless, challenging. The issues they present are intended to engage the intellectual curiosity of all readers whether or not they are already familiar with the particular subject areas covered.

In addition, the selections are long enough to engage the reader to the point at which full understanding becomes likely.

What Sorts of Activities Are Included?

In order that it have the best possible chance for becoming internalized, content must be explored in sufficient depth so that the reader can experience its presence, reflect upon its substance, and expand upon its meaning. The activities are an attempt to aid in this process. In addition, they are intended to help students become skilled readers at academic levels by increasing their basic comprehension and speed. The latter is accomplished not through the pressure of time (i.e., timed readings) but through increased understanding and the ability to pinpoint major ideas and concepts and to see relationships among them.

All the units begin with prereading questions that act as starters to get students into the topic and to help them relate to prior knowledge and experience. Through this means, key concepts are introduced. In addition to prereading questions, the teacher might list a few key words on the chalkboard or on an overhead transparency. The students can then say anything that comes to mind relating to these words while the teacher records the associations for all to see and asks questions to clarify and/or extend meaning.

In most cases, prereading activities also include anticipation statements about the content of the reading. Students are asked to prejudge the validity of these statements. Motivation to read is aroused as the students begin to seek out information that will either support or refute their preconceived notions. In addition, teachers might call students' attention to titles, pictures, headings, and any other features that could offer clues to the content.

By means of the activities following each selection, higher order thinking skills are expected to evolve progressively. Each unit begins at the knowledge level and moves slowly toward more demanding, less context-embedded ways of thinking and operating. Each unit builds upon the preceding ones as the students stretch to increasingly higher levels. Eventually, the students begin to gain confidence in their abilities to analyze, synthesize, and evaluate what they read.

Each unit ends with ideas for discussion and writing which take the students beyond the text and the classroom, often to other settings and other resources.

Most of the activities and ideas can be easily modified in whatever ways seem appropriate. Those meant for discussion can often be written, and vice versa. Those intended for pair work can be adapted for use with larger groups. It should also be emphasized that students who do not feel comfortable with a particular activity, for whatever reason, should not be required to participate. Activities not considered culturally appropriate or not suited to the particular needs of specific groups should be eliminated altogether.

How Are the Units Organized?

The units have been arranged so as to maximize the students' feelings of success. Important considerations included (1) natural reinforcement of concepts, structures, and skills and (2) difficulty levels, both semantic and syntactic. However, because judgments in these matters are complicated and highly subjective, the prudent teacher will not feel bound to the present arrangement but will change it as he or she sees fit. In addition, not all units need to be included. The decision of whether or not to include a specific unit should be based on students' needs and interests.

Does the Teacher Need Special Training or Knowledge in the Content Areas Represented?

The answer to this is "no." Any teacher with a general education or liberal arts background can feel comfortable with the materials. Because the selections are nontechnical, they can be enjoyed by large numbers of students and their teachers. Even the unit on mathematics can be pleasurable for "nonmath" persons. It must be remembered too that much information can be shared. The teacher does not have to be the "expert" in all areas. Instead he or she can serve as a guide and facilitator, bringing out the best in everyone and allowing everyone to be an expert at one time or another.

Whether students are working on activities alone or in groups, the teacher can circulate among them, showing a keen interest in what they are doing, gaining insight into their perspectives and understandings, and offering guidance when necessary.

How Should New Vocabulary Be Approached?

As mentioned above, key concepts are generally presented in the prereading activities. However, the students will need effective strategies to enable them to deal with other unfamiliar vocabulary within the readings themselves.*

In most situations the following strategies appear to work best. Encourage the student to:

1. *Read*   Read each selection through first, without consciously stopping to figure out every unfamiliar word or phrase. Remember that good readers look for overall meaning and are not concerned about every new element. New words and phrases often become clear from understanding the context in which they are found.

2. *Reread for Greater Understanding*   When finished with the first reading of the selection, go back and read it again. This time make a more conscious effort to guess the meaning of words and phrases that remain puzzling. Write in pencil some of the guesses above or beside each word or phrase. Return to the context for clues. At this point, it may be necessary to check the "Definitions and Clues" box at the bottom of the page for the word or phrase.

3. *Discuss and/or Look Up Unfamiliar Elements*   In a case in which a particular word or phrase is still unclear, discuss it with another member of the class or with the teacher. Or look it up in a dictionary. Note that in the dictionary several different meanings may be given. Refer back to the context to make sure you have chosen the appropriate one.

* One word of caution here. If there appear to be too many unfamiliar elements for particular students, they may need to be given lower-level materials at first. See other titles in the Longman series.

What About Reading Aloud?

Forcing students to read aloud often interferes with the normal reading process and creates anxiety. Reading aloud is a very specialized skill that should be attempted only by volunteers and only after the selection has been read silently and its meaning comprehended. Exceptions include easily understood stories, plays, poetry, and other pieces read by the teacher, other experienced readers, or volunteers. Remember, however, that in most situations reading is a very personal activity and requires uninterrupted time in a quiet, comfortable, nonthreatening atmosphere either at home or in the classroom.

Conclusion

The book aims to provide pleasurable experiences in academic reading through an interactive approach to skills development. The teacher can facilitate the process by providing a supportive environment in which students explore their inner resources in relation to the content and to one another, thereby reaching higher and higher levels of understanding.

TO THE STUDENT

The book introduces you to academic readings in ten areas: sociology, art, music, business, natural science, history, literature, anthropology, mathematics, and psychology. The readings are from current textbooks used in college and university classes on English-speaking campuses. You will be asked to think about questions such as these: What does it mean to be creative? Is it possible to be truly "equal" in a society? What kinds of things do people think about when facing death? and many more.

The activities before and after each reading will help you discover meaning at several different levels. They will aid you in developing many of the skills needed for survival in college and university classrooms. Forming your own opinions and supporting them, increasing your vocabulary, organizing information, applying knowledge, and using techniques to aid memory are only a few of the skill areas in which you will work. Some activities ask for the bare facts about the reading. But most of them, in one way or another, ask you to think about the reading in relation to your own life and the lives of others around you. During many activities you will work alone. During others you will work with a partner or a small group. Your teacher will serve as your guide.

While you are on this journey into academic readings, it is hoped that you will improve your reading and thinking skills in English not through drill and exercises but through understanding and reflection. The book has been designed for your pleasure as well as for your learning.

ACKNOWLEDGMENTS

I wish to thank the many people who directly or indirectly contributed to the development of this book. Alice Lyons-Quinn from the Center for English Language and Orientation Programs at Boston University offered numerous insightful comments and suggestions. Sue Gould and Wendy Hansen, both former reading teachers, critiqued the manuscript in its early stages and contributed many helpful ideas. Mary McGroarty from Northern Arizona University helped make arrangements for field testing. Sharyn Moore at the ELS Language Center in Santa Monica field-tested a representative portion of the materials and gave valuable suggestions. Leslie Jo Adams willingly shared her knowledge and part of her library with me. Jennifer Claire Johnson proofread the final manuscript. Joanne Dresner, Penny Laporte, and the other editors at Longman gave very helpful advice, especially in the book's final stages. The staff at the University Square Bookstore at Cal State, Los Angeles, graciously loaned me textbooks out of which many of the selections came. And Jay, my husband, encouraged me throughout the project.

READING
IN THE CONTENT AREAS

Unit 1 / Sociology

A SOCIOLOGICAL PERSPECTIVE

Being alone, away from society, is feared by some people and longed for by others. Have you ever been separated from other people for a period of time? Perhaps you were on a camping trip or stationed in a place far away from a city or town. Were you completely alone? How many people were with you? How long did you stay? Describe your experience. To what extent did you feel independent? To what extent did you feel lonely?

Now look at the title of the reading on page 4. What do you think a "sociological" perspective or viewpoint might be? How might such a viewpoint help to explain the way humans behave? How might it differ from other perspectives? Consider, for example, a "biological" perspective or a "psychological" perspective.

Read the three statements below. Write whether you agree or disagree with each statement and briefly explain why.

a. We can be completely independent from society if that is what we really want. It's a matter of choice.

_____

_____

_____

b. A person who is alone might not laugh even if he or she thinks something is funny.

_____

_____

_____

c. A person who usually cares about personal appearance may not care when persons of the opposite sex are not around.

_____

_____

_____

People sometimes take society for granted. They may forget what an important role it plays not only in their emotional well-being but also in their everyday behavior. Often it is when people are alone for long periods of time that they fully realize what it means to be part of society.

A Sociological Perspective

DONALD A. HOBBS
AND STUART J. BLANK

"No man is an island, entire of itself; every man is a piece of the continent, a part of the main."

John Donne, 1623

We are all involved in humankind. From birth to death each person participates in society. Neither an individual nor any human experience can be understood independently of the individual's involvement with other humans. We cannot exaggerate the importance of people to people. Imagine completely removing yourself from the ties of family, friends, and all other people too. Alone and isolated, imagine what your thoughts, feelings, and actions might be. No one has ever existed totally independent of society. But some people have experienced different degrees of independence. The famous explorer of the Antarctic, Admiral

Byrd, voluntarily isolated himself for several months in a polar region. In that isolation, he experienced what we consider to be a basic sociological truth. In his diary Byrd wrote that solitude is an excellent state in which to observe how much our behavior is influenced by others. He said that much of what we take for granted through contacts with others becomes painfully apparent in isolation. According to Byrd, even laughter no longer is apt to occur when one is so isolated: " . . . now when I laugh, I laugh inside; for I seem to have forgotten how to do it out loud." He wrote that laughing aloud is mostly a way to share pleasure. In our everyday relations with other people, great importance is attached to physical appearance. In isolation, Byrd wrote, physical appearance seems to have little significance: "Looking in the mirror . . . I decided that a man without women around him is a man without vanity . . . how I look is no longer of the least importance; all that matters is how I feel" (Byrd, 1938).

The *sociological perspective* is a point of view that most, if not all, human behavior involves others either directly or indirectly. In fact, most of our individual behavior is not purely individualistic. Humans, as social beings, do not live in a social vacuum.

THE RELATIONSHIP OF THE INDIVIDUAL TO SOCIETY

For a long time scholars have debated over different views about the relationship be-

---

Definitions and Clues

polar: Located near the North or South poles.

solitude: Being by oneself (*soli-* refers to being alone).

vanity: The condition of being vain or showing too much attention to appearance.

tween an individual and society. Does a person control the conditions of society? Or do the conditions of society control the person? Does an individual have free will? Is a person free to become what he or she chooses? Or is a person more controlled by society—even a rubber stamp of society? These are the kinds of questions that the scholars have debated. Those who see the person as an independent being who makes decisions and acts freely are called *individual determinists*. Those who see the person as acting always under the influence and control of society are called *social determinists* (Vernon, 1965).

The views of people presented by individual determinists and by social determinists seem to conflict. However, sociologists would say that both are somewhat correct, but neither is entirely correct. It makes no sense to separate the individual and society: one does not—cannot—exist without the other. The sociological perspective is that each person is part of society. Society is made up of people who influence one another in many ways. We know that individuals make choices and decisions. But the kinds of choices and decisions they make are limited by their experiences and involvement in society.

Consider the relationships within a family unit consisting of a husband, a wife, and a child. A husband influences his wife and his child. A wife influences her husband and her child. The child influences its mother and its father. Add another child. A grandparent. Another grandparent. Add an aunt. And an uncle. Add a cousin. Another cousin. A neighbor. Friends. Co-workers. If we were to expand this list we would end up with an entire society. A society is a network of relationships among individuals. Each will influence others,

and each will be influenced by others. This is social interaction. Social interaction is at the very heart of the human experience.

SOCIAL INTERACTION

The unique perspective that sociology has is that the most basic and significant of all human behavior is *social interaction*. People need people. This is the supreme fact of the human experience. Human beings are social beings. What we love and hope for or hate and fear are experienced because of our involvement with others.

Social interaction occurs when people take each other into account and influence one another. Checking out at the supermarket requires social interaction. Playing baseball is social interaction. What happens at school, at work, and at home all involve social interaction if two or more people have influences on the others involved in the activity. In day-to-day life, a person meets people, competes with them or cooperates with them, agrees or disagrees with them, laughs with them or at them. In all such cases, social interaction takes place. Some social bonds are strong and lasting. Others are weak and here today, gone tomorrow. Some social relationships, such as marriage or friendship, can last all through one's life. All kinds of social bonds are based on social interaction.

We simply cannot avoid the fact that each of us is bound in some degree to other people. Despite our single savage selves, despite our unique individualism, despite the idea of individual determinism, each person feels, thinks, and acts as a result of social interaction with other human beings.

Definitions and Clues

network: Having interconnected lines (like a net).
savage: Wild.
unique: One of a kind (*uni-* refers to one).

Checking Your Prereading Reactions

Return to the statements on page 3. Look again at your reactions. Discuss whether your ideas have changed after reading "A Sociological Perspective."

Understanding Intended Meaning

Discuss the following questions with your class.

1. How important do the authors think society is to the individual? Relate your answer to the quote by John Donne that begins this reading.

2. What basic sociological truth did Admiral Byrd discover?

3. According to a sociological perspective, what is the most basic human behavior? Explain.

Determining the Theme

The theme or underlying idea of a reading is a statement of what the author is trying to say. Often themes are not stated directly but are discovered by the reader. Check the statement below that you feel comes closest to the main theme expressed in this reading. Discuss your choice with the class.

1. People in isolation often realize for the first time how important society is to their lives.

2. All humans are influenced to a greater extent than most realize by the society in which they live.

3. Social interaction occurs when humans come into contact with one another.

4. Some social relationships last a lifetime and others are only temporary.

Discovering Opposing Viewpoints Through Comparison

The authors briefly compare two opposing viewpoints about the relationship of the individual to society: the viewpoint of the individual determinist and that of the social determinist. Reread the section dealing with these two viewpoints. In a few words, describe each one below.

The Individual Determinist	The Social Determinist

With which viewpoint do you agree most? Discuss your answer with your classmates.

Drawing on Personal Experience

Discuss the following with a classmate.

1. Consider Admiral Byrd's reactions to his isolation. Think about his inability to laugh out loud. Think about his lack of vanity because he was not around members of the opposite sex. Do you think you would have similar reactions? Why or why not?

2. The authors ask us to consider the many personal relationships we have. Think of two or three specific people who have had the most influence on your life. Include people such as your mother, father, spouse, grandparent, cousin, other relatives, or close friends. Describe briefly what the influence of each has been.

3. The authors write: "We know that individuals make choices and decisions. But the kinds of choices and decisions they make are limited by their experiences and involvement in society" (page 5). Recall a choice or decision that you have had to make recently. To what extent do you think it may have been limited by society as a whole?

Comparing Cultural Expectations

We are not always aware of the limits that society places upon us. We just know when a certain behavior "feels" right or "feels" wrong according to our cultural backgrounds. Often, cultures differ in their expectations. For example, in some cultures it is necessary to be on time to particular events. In other cultures, being on time is not generally considered that important. One can arrive an hour or two late and not be considered rude. Think of ways in which the expectations of the culture with which you are most familiar seem to be in conflict with those of another culture. Write your ideas below and then share them with classmates to see whether or not they agree.

The culture with which I am most familiar	Another culture
Example:	
Name of the culture: *Chinese*	Name of the culture: *Canadian*
Expectation: *It is rude to talk openly about myself.*	Expectation: *I am often encouraged to talk openly about myself.*
Name of the culture: _____	Name of the culture: _____
Expectations: _____ _____ _____ _____	Expectations: _____ _____ _____ _____

Interviewing a Partner

Ask a partner the following questions about social issues. You can write your own questions for numbers 3 and 4.

1.   In your opinion, what makes some social bonds last longer than others?

2.   Think about the roles of men and women in society. Do you think that men and women should share roles equally in the following areas?

► on the job
► in the household
► in the army

3.   _____

4.   _____

Ideas for Discussion and/or Writing

1.   Begin a journal in which you make entries two or three times a week. Include your reflections on experiences with others, the insights you gain into human social behavior through these experiences, and anything else you may want to write. You may want to share your journal with your teacher from time to time.

2.   Find a book of quotations in your school or university library. Your teacher or the librarian may be able to help you. From the book, select a quotation about a social aspect of human behavior you find to be particularly significant. For example, you might be struck by something as simple as "To have a friend, you must be a friend." Develop your ideas using the quotation as the topic. You may want to tell what the quote means to you and apply its meaning to your own life and/or the lives of others.

3.   Use your list of cultural expectations on page 7 to develop a comparison of the two cultures.

4.   Choose one of the questions from Interviewing a Partner on this page. Develop your ideas using the question as the topic. Apply it to your own life.

5.   Choose a book or a short story about someone isolated from society. Below are some suggestions. After reading, think about the new insights you have gained.

Alive (book) by Piers Paul Read
   The true story of the survivors of a plane crash in the high Andes of South America.

Alone (book) by Admiral Byrd
   An account of an explorer's personal experiences in the Antarctic where he manned a weather base.

Island of Blue Dolphins (book) by Scott O'Dell
   A Native American woman lived alone for more than 20 years on an island off the coast of California. This book describes her life.

"To Build a Fire" (story) by Jack London
   A fictional story of a man alone who braves the cold and struggles against almost certain death.

Unit 2 / Art

CREATIVITY

Pablo Picasso.
HEAD (study for GUERNICA). May 24, 1937.
Pencil and gouache. 11 3/8″ × 9¼″.
The Prado, Madrid.

What is creative to one person may not be considered so by another. Much depends on one's perspective. Look at the picture on the preceding page. Do you think it is creative? Why or why not? How would you define the word "creativity"?

Think about the quote that begins the reading selection on page 11. Do you agree or disagree with it?

Read the following statements. Check the ones you think are true.

a. People need to stop playing around and start working before they can come up with creative ideas.

b. The creative process follows a general pattern and is the same for most people.

c. To be truly creative one must begin with ideas that have never existed before.

d. Children should be taught as early as possible to create the way adults do. In this way they will create things of high quality sooner.

The authors of the following selection describe the creative process and present the major characteristics of creative people. They also speak of a "cultural tragedy" that has taken place in our society. Find out what this tragedy is and what we can do to prevent it.

CREATIVITY

DUANE PREBLE AND SARAH PREBLE

" . . . a first-rate soup is more creative than a second-rate painting."

Abraham Maslow, 1968

Creativity often begins when the creator is struck with an idea or faced with a problem. It can also be the result of playing or "fooling around." In fact, play can be as important to adult creativity as it is to child development. Playful activity is a kind of sportive, open-ended toying with possibilities. During play a creative person is alert to the unexpected, yet significant, promise of chance events.

There are as many ways to create as there are creative people, but creative processes generally have certain sequential characteristics in common. Dr. G. Wallis' thorough study of creativity led to his four-stage theory of the creative process.[1] (We include his theory here only to suggest some important components of the creative process. In actuality, the process will not necessarily follow or even include all of these stages.)

During the first stage, *preparation,* one en-thusiastically collects data and media. Excitement, questioning, study, and perplexity often affect one's mood at this stage.

Incubation is the second stage. There is a shift from the conscious to the unconscious; one may relax and turn to other things. During this period the metaphorical mind takes over and visual images realign themselves. Incubation is considered to be the most important phase. One may have sudden, incomplete insights.

Wallis calls the third stage *illumination.* During this stage, the solution suddenly appears, often unexpectedly. One "knows" this is the long-awaited inspiration. A feeling of certainty and joy pervades one's entire being. The visual artist may quickly sketch the design, the composer may record a few bars of music, the poet may write the central lines of a new poem, and the scientist may jot down notes for a whole new line of research.

Verification or *revision* is the fourth stage. The artist works out the design and completes the final form, the scientist completes experiments and presents the proven theory. This

Definitions and Clues

perplexity: The state of being puzzled (to perplex means to puzzle or confuse).

incubation: A controlled environment for development.

illumination: Casting light, making something clear.

pervades: Spreads throughout (*per-* here means completely; *-vades* refers to going in). Consider also the meaning of "one's entire being" in the same sentence.

verification: Additional evidence to support the truth of . . .

stage culminates in the presentation of the newly created form.

To be creative is to be able to put existing things together in original ways, thus producing a new object, image, or idea.

Studies of creativity have produced various descriptions of the major characteristics of creative people. These include the abilities to:

▶ wonder, be curious

▶ be enthusiastic, spontaneous, and flexible

▶ be willing to approach new experience with an open mind and to see the familiar from an unfamiliar point of view

▶ confront complexity and ambiguity with interest

▶ take advantage of accidental events in order to make desirable but unsought discoveries (called serendipity)

▶ make one thing out of another by shifting its functions

▶ generalize in order to see universal applications of ideas

▶ synthesize and integrate, find order in disorder

▶ be in touch with unconscious sources yet be intensely conscious

▶ visualize or imagine new possibilities

▶ be analytical and critical

▶ know oneself, have the courage to be oneself in the face of opposition, and be willing to take risks

▶ be willing to "lose" oneself in one's work

▶ be persistent, working for long periods in pursuit of a goal, without guaranteed results.

Nearly all children have rich, creative imaginations. They naturally reach out to the world around them from birth. They taste, touch, hear, see, and smell their environment, becoming part of it through their senses. All forms of expressive communication are part of that reaching out. Children who are confronted with experiences that indicate their experiments are of questionable value soon stop reaching so far.

Most of the abilities listed as being characteristic of creative people are found in children during the first few years of life. What happens to this extraordinary capacity? According to John Holt, author of *How Children Fail,*

We destroy this capacity above all by making them afraid—afraid of not doing what other people want, of not pleasing, or of making mistakes, of failing, or being wrong. Thus we make them afraid to gamble, afraid to experiment, afraid to try the difficult and unknown.[2]

Many people, including some parents and teachers, may—without realizing the consequences—ignore and even attack evidence of creative imagination in children. This destructiveness can be traced to their own underdeveloped imaginations and to a cycle of ignorance and anxiety regarding creativity that has been passed on for generations. We tend to

---

Definitions and Clues

culminates: Reaches the highest point or degree (*culmin-* refers to the peak).

spontaneous: Unplanned.

ambiguity: Confusion of meaning (*ambi-* refers to having more than one).

synthesize: To blend together (*synthe-* refers to putting things together). Consider also the meaning of "integrate."

discourage in others what has been discouraged in ourselves. Yet to ignore or to belittle expressive work is to say, "Your experience is not valid, therefore, you are not valid."

For all of us, especially the very young, mental and emotional growth depends on our ability to integrate our experience of the outside world with that of our inner selves. For this reason opportunities for creative expression are extremely important. The art process helps us to discover and confirm ourselves and our relations with our world.

Obviously, all of us have been children, and most will be parents. Not so obviously, many attitudes about art are shaped during childhood. Because artistic efforts are more personal than many other kinds of work, children as well as adults tend to be particularly vulnerable to disparaging remarks about such efforts. Even comments that may not be intentionally critical or negative may be perceived as such, and thus may be very intimidating. This is why it is essential for adults to examine what happens to artistic development in children.

Young children depict the world in symbolic rather than realistic ways. Children's art is seen as inferior only when children and others want their work to look like photographs or works produced by adults. This dissatisfaction usually occurs around age nine or ten, and frequently results in a lifetime of blocked creativity. Many of those who succeed in making the transition from children's art to adult art find it painful. The majority make the transition visually, but not artistically. They learn to see the world in terms of adult conventions, but are unable to create corresponding images. They become frustrated because they cannot draw the way they have learned to see. This is a cultural tragedy.

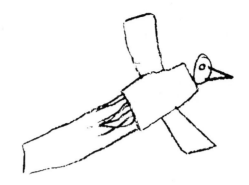

BIRDS
a. This bird shows one child's expression before exposure to coloring books.

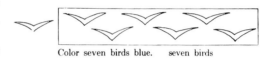

Color seven birds blue.   seven birds

b. Then the child colored a workbook illustration.

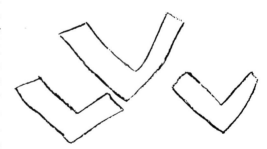

c. After coloring the workbook birds, the child lost creative sensitivity and self-reliance.

Definitions and Clues

vulnerable: Unprotected from harm.
disparaging: Degrading.
symbolic: Is used to represent something else.

It has long been recognized by researchers in art education that most children who have been given coloring books, workbooks, and predrawn printed single sheets at home and in school become dependent on such stereotyped, impersonal props. They lose the urge to invent unique images relevant to their own experience, as well as individual modes of expression for those images. Such devices may even block the development of discipline and skills. Without opportunities for relevant personal expression, the urge to achieve or excel can be lost.

It is important that children be given the opportunity to give honest, tangible expression to their ideas, feelings, and experiences. Adults as well as children need a great deal of encouragement to be able to express themselves without fear or hesitation.

Self-assurance shows clearly in this self-portrait by a 4-year-old girl. The line drawn around the edge of her paper shows an awareness of the whole space. One hand with radi-

Malia, age 4.
SELF-PORTRAIT.

ating fingers reaches out, giving strong asymmetrical balance to the composition. This was accomplished spontaneously after considerable drawing experience, but without any adult guidance or conscious knowledge of design.

Children nearly always demonstrate an innate sense of design. We lose this intuitive sense of balanced composition as we begin to look at the world from a learned, conceptual point of view. As adults, we must rediscover our innate sensitivity to design. Referring to this intuitive ability, Picasso is alleged to have said that he could always draw like Michelangelo, but it took him years to draw like a child.

For people of all ages, the creative process provides a way of objectifying personal experience and thereby building personal identity and self-confidence. Artistic problems have many equally "correct" solutions. Each person—child or adult—has the opportunity to create work that is unlike anyone else's, and different from what that person has previously created. Discovering the potential for many "right" answers is very healthy. In this way the arts complement and facilitate all other aspects of a person's education.

Our attention to art as a means of self-discovery is not intended to suggest that the purpose of art is merely self-expression, or that art is easy and therefore everyone should dabble in it. Art gives us courage to go deeper into ourselves, beyond our personalities to something universal. The potential for art is in everyone, but discipline and considerable effort are often necessary before it can be expressed. Ability is nothing unless it is developed, focused, and acted upon with commitment.

Definitions and Clues

stereotyped: Given a fixed, often overly simplified treatment.

tangible: Capable of being touched (*tang-* refers to touch).

asymmetrical: The two halves are not the same (*a-* here means not).

innate: Inborn (*in-* means within; *-nate* refers to born).

Checking Your Prereading Reactions

Return to the statements on page 10. Look again at your reactions. Discuss whether your ideas have changed after reading "Creativity."

Understanding Intended Meaning

Discuss the following questions with your class.

1.   At the beginning of the reading, the authors mention the conditions that are important to creativity. What are they? Include any specific examples you can think of that might illustrate these conditions.

2.   In what ways is it possible for adults to "play"?

3.   Refer to the last two paragraphs of the reading selection. What do the authors feel are the benefits of the creative process to individuals in society?

4.   Can you think of any other benefits? Make a list.

Determining the Theme

In Unit 1 the theme or underlying idea of a reading was defined as "a statement of what the author is trying to say." Write a statement below that you feel expresses the theme of this reading.

_____

_____

Discuss it with your classmates. You may want to make some changes in your statement based on what you learn from the discussion.

Using a Chart to Clarify a Process

Dr. G. Wallis, in defining the process of creativity (see page 11), claims that there are four stages through which a person moves during the creative process. Complete the chart with information from the text.

Stage	Description
1.	*Data and media are collected.*
2. *Incubation*	
3.	
4.	

Exploring a Problem and Its Solution

Discuss the following questions with your class.

1. What societal problem do the authors call a "cultural tragedy" (see page 13)? Describe it in your own words.

2. Why do the authors think this cultural tragedy occurs?

3. Do you remember any personal experiences in your early schooling that may have affected your own ability to create?

4. What do the authors suggest we can do to help children develop their creativity? Do you agree or disagree? Before arriving at your answer, consider the drawings on page 13 and the portion of the text that refers to them.

Relating the Text to Cultural Background

Does this tragedy also occur in the culture with which you are most familiar? Discuss your ideas with your classmates.

Giving Reasons for the Choices You Make

Of all of the characteristics of creative people listed on page 12, which three do you consider most important? Discuss them with a classmate. Give reasons for your choices.

Ideas for Discussion and/or Writing

1. Choose one of the characteristics of creative people from the list on page 12. Give specific examples from your own life, or those of others, to show how this particular characteristic is necessary to creativity.

2. Bring to class a favorite work of art or a photo of one. Discuss why you feel it is creative.

3. Develop three or four questions to ask people in order to find out about their likes and dislikes in art. You might want to show them pictures or other art objects to which you can relate your questions. Interview several people on your school campus and come back to class ready to share what you have learned.

4. React to the following quote taken from page 14: "Art gives us courage to go deeper into ourselves, beyond our personalities to something universal." In your discussion, include what you think the role of art might be in bringing cultures together in harmony.

5. Visit a local art gallery. Decide which pieces of art are your favorites. Come back to class ready to discuss or write about them.

Notes

1. Mike Samuels and Nancy Samuels, *Seeing with the Mind's Eye* (New York: Random House and Berkeley, CA: The Bookworks, 1975), p. 239.

2. John Holt, *How Children Fail* (New York: Pitman, 1964), p. 167. Reprinted with permission.

Unit 3 / Music

THE FAMOUS DEAF COMPOSER: LUDWIG VAN BEETHOVEN

Ludwig van Beethoven

Seeing a person overcome a disability to achieve his or her goals gives all of us hope that we too can reach our potential. How do you think a composer such as Beethoven could continue his work after becoming deaf? Do you know of others who have overcome disabilities to continue their life's work?

Music has always had a powerful effect on people. Sometimes it soothes hurt feelings; other times it brings great joy. What effects do some kinds of music have on you? Why?

Now listen to a recording of Beethoven's music. Perhaps your teacher or a member of your class can bring in a record or a tape to share. After listening to a segment of the music, think about how it makes you feel. Later you will have a chance to compare it to other kinds of music.

It is difficult to imagine how a musician can compose music after becoming deaf, just as it is difficult to imagine how an artist can paint pictures after becoming blind. Find out how Ludwig van Beethoven, in spite of his deafness, went on to become one of the world's greatest composers.

The Famous Deaf Composer: Ludwig van Beethoven

ROGER KAMIEN

For many people, Ludwig van Beethoven (1770–1827) represents the highest level of musical genius. His unique stature is comparable to Shakespeare's[1] in literature and Michelangelo's[2] in art. He opened new realms of musical expression that profoundly influenced composers throughout the nineteenth century.

Beethoven was born on December 16, 1770, in Bonn, Germany. Like Bach[3] and Mozart[4] before him, he came from a family of musicians. His grandfather, also named Ludwig, was music director of the court at Bonn. His father, Johann, was a tenor who held a low position in the court and who saw his talented son as a profitable prodigy like Mozart. It's told that Johann Beethoven and a musician friend would come home from the local tavern late at night, rouse young Ludwig from sleep, and make him practice at the keyboard until morning. At eleven, Beethoven served as assistant to the court organist, and by thirteen he had several piano compositions published.

Beethoven went to Vienna when he was sixteen to improvise for Mozart, who said, "Keep your eyes on him; some day he will give the world something to talk about." He then returned to Bonn because his mother was critically ill. She died shortly after, and his father, who became an alcoholic, was dismissed from the court choir. Beethoven, at eighteen, became legal guard-

---

Definitions and Clues

tenor: A man who sings in a high but natural male voice.

prodigy: A person with exceptional talents (*prodig-* refers to a thing of wonder).

rouse: To awaken.

improvise: To invent without preparation. Here *im-* means not; *-provise* refers to foreseen or planned.

critically: In this case it means of utmost importance.

ian of two younger brothers. At court he was organist and violist, composing and practicing; suddenly, he was also head of a family.

Shortly before his twenty-second birthday, Beethoven left Bonn to study with Haydn[5] in Vienna, where he spent the rest of his life. In 1792, Haydn was at the height of his fame, too busy composing to devote much time or energy to teaching. As a result, he overlooked errors in Beethoven's counterpoint exercises, and his pupil felt forced to go secretly to another teacher. (Haydn never learned of this.) Beethoven's drive for thoroughness and mastery—evident throughout his life—is shown by his willingness to subject himself to a strict course in counterpoint and fugue even after he had composed fine works.

Beethoven's first seven years in Vienna brought hard work, growing confidence, a strong sense of identity, and public praise. His letters of introduction from Bonn noblemen opened the doors of the social and cultural elite in this music-loving city. He dazzled everyone with his piano virtuosity and moved them with his improvisations. "He knew how to produce such an impression on every listener," reports a contemporary, "that frequently there was not a single dry eye, while many broke out into loud sobs, for there was a certain magic in his expression." A rebel against social convention, Beethoven asserted that an artist deserved as much respect as nobles. Once, while playing in an aristocratic drawing room, he was disturbed by the loud conversation of a young count. Beethoven jumped up from the piano, exclaiming, "I will not play for such swine!"

Disaster struck during his twenty-ninth year: Beethoven felt the first symptoms of deafness. Doctors could do nothing to halt the course of his physical and emotional torment. In 1801 he wrote despairingly, "For two years I have avoided almost all social gatherings because it is impossible for me to say to people 'I am deaf.' If I belonged to any other profession it would be easier, but in my profession it is a dreadful state." On October 6, 1802, Beethoven was in Heiligenstadt, a village outside Vienna where he sought solitude during the summer. That day his feelings were expressed in what is now known as the Heiligenstadt Testament, a long, agonized letter addressed to his brothers. Beethoven wrote, "I would have ended my life—it was only my art that held me back. Ah, it seemed to me impossible to leave the world until I had brought forth all that I felt was within me."

Beethoven's victory over despair coincided with an important change in his musical style. Works created after his emotional crisis have a new power and heroism. From 1803 to 1804, he composed the gigantic Third Symphony, the *Eroica,* a landmark in music history. At first, he planned to name it "Bonaparte," after the first consul of the French Republic. Beethoven saw

---

Definitions and Clues

violist: A person who plays a viola, a four-string instrument larger than a violin.

counterpoint: A contrasting melody added above or below an existing melody (counter means against).

fugue: Music using counterpoint and building in stages to a high point.

virtuosity: The skill shown by one who is very talented (a virtuoso).

convention: Here it means custom.

aristocratic: From the upper class in society.

consul: A high official in government.

Napoleon as the embodiment of heroism and the champion of the principles underlying the French Revolution. "Liberty, equality, fraternity" were stirring words that expressed Beethoven's democratic ideals. But when he learned that Napoleon had proclaimed himself emperor of the French, Beethoven "flew into a rage and cried out, 'He too is nothing but an ordinary man! Now he will trample under foot all the rights of man and only indulge his ambition. He will exalt himself above all others and become a tyrant!'" Seizing his score, Beethoven tore out the title page bearing Napoleon's name and threw it on the floor. On a new title page, later, Beethoven wrote, "Heroic Symphony composed to celebrate the memory of a great man."

In 1812, Beethoven met Johann Wolfgang von Goethe, the great German poet he had long worshiped. He played for Goethe and the two artists walked and talked together. Shortly after this meeting, Goethe described Beethoven to a friend as "an utterly untamed personality." To his wife the poet wrote, "Never before have I seen an artist with more power of concentration, more energy, more inwardness." Despite such descriptions by people who knew him, Beethoven remains a mystery. He was self-educated and had read widely in Shakespeare and the ancient classics, but he was weak in elementary arithmetic. He claimed the highest moral principles, but he was often unscrupulous in dealing with publishers. Orderly and methodical when composing, Beethoven dressed sloppily and lived in incredibly messy apartments. During his thirty-five years in Vienna, he changed dwellings about forty times.

Beethoven fell in and out of love with several women, mostly of noble birth, but never was able to form a lasting relationship. To a woman referred to as "the Immortal Beloved," he wrote a passionate letter that was found in a drawer after his death. Only recently has a Beethoven scholar established her identity as the Viennese aristocrat Antonie Brentano. Beethoven took consolation from nature for disappointments in his personal life. Ideas came to him while walking through the Viennese countryside. His Sixth Symphony, the "Pastoral," beautifully expresses his recollections of life in the country.

As Beethoven's hearing weakened, so did his piano playing and conducting. By the age of forty-four, this once brilliant pianist was forced to stop playing in public. But he insisted on conducting his orchestral works long after he could do it efficiently. The players would become

---

Definitions and Clues

embodiment: That which gives bodily form to something (*em-* means in; *-bod-* refers to body).

fraternity: Brotherhood (*frater-* refers to brothers).

proclaimed: Cried out (*pro-* means forth or forward; *-claim-* refers to cry out).

exalt: To honor (*ex-* in this case means up; *-alt* refers to high). "Above all others" is a clue.

tyrant: A harsh, forceful person (*tyran-* refers to being harsh).

unscrupulous: Not having a sense of right or wrong (*un-* means not; a scruple is a sense of right or wrong).

methodical: Following steps in an organized fashion (a method involves a set of steps).

immortal: Living forever (*im-* here means not; *-mort-* refers to dying).

consolation: A comfort (to console means to comfort).

confused by his wild gestures on the podium, and performances were often chaotic. His sense of isolation grew with his deafness. Friends had to communicate with him through an ear trumpet, and during his last eight years he carried notebooks in which people would write questions and comments.

In 1815, his brother Caspar died, and Beethoven and the widow became coguardians of the nine-year-old son. Young Carl was the object of a savage tug-of-war. For five years, Beethoven fought legal battles for exclusive custody of his nephew; he finally won. This "victory" was a disaster for everyone. Growing up in the household of a deaf, eccentric bachelor uncle is not easy at best, and for Carl it was complicated by Beethoven's craving for love and companionship. The young man attempted suicide, a crushing event for Beethoven, whose health was already poor.

During the first three years of legal battles over Carl, Beethoven composed less, and the Viennese began to whisper that he was finished. Beethoven heard the rumor and said, "Wait a while, they'll soon learn differently!" And they did. After 1818, Beethoven's domestic problems did not prevent a creative outburst that produced some of his greatest works: the late piano sonatas and string quartets, the *Missa solemnis,* and the Ninth Symphony—out of total deafness, new realms of sounds.

BEETHOVEN'S MUSIC

"I must despise the world which does not know that music is a higher revelation than all wisdom and philosophy." For Beethoven, music was not mere entertainment, but a moral force capable of creating a vision of higher ideals. His music directly reflects his powerful, tortured personality. In both art and life, his heroic struggle resulted in victory over despair.

Beethoven's demand for perfection meant long and hard work. Unlike Mozart, he couldn't dash off three great symphonies in six weeks. Sometimes he worked years on a single symphony, writing other works at the same time. He carried music sketchbooks everywhere, jotting down new ideas, revising and refining old ones. These early notes often seem crude and uninspired when compared with their final versions, which were hammered out through great labor.

Definitions and Clues

chaotic: Chaos means a state of complete disorder.

ear trumpet: A cone-shaped device used to direct sound; an old version of a hearing aid.

eccentric: Different from the usual (*ec-* refers to out; *-centric* refers to center).

sonatas: Musical compositions with three or four very different stages.

quartets: Music for four instruments or musicians (*qua-* means four).

revelation: Something brought into view (relates to the word "reveal").

Understanding Intended Meaning

Discuss the following questions with your class.

1. What did Beethoven's father do to him that most people would consider cruel?

2. What were Beethoven's first seven years in Vienna like? Include the reaction of the people to his music.

3. In what way was Beethoven "a rebel against social convention"? (See page 21.)

4. What was Beethoven's reaction to his increasing deafness? How did it affect his music?

5. In what ways did Beethoven remain a mystery to those who appreciated his music?

6. How would you describe his relationships, especially with women? How did he console himself?

7. What was his relationship with his nephew? Describe the legal "tug-of-war" over his nephew and its effect on both of them.

8. How did Beethoven react to rumors that his career as a composer was over?

Distinguishing Fact from Opinion

A fact is a statement that can be supported by evidence that is generally accepted as true. An opinion, on the other hand, is a statement with which others might disagree, depending upon their point of view.

   Read each statement and decide if it is fact or opinion. Write *fact* or *opinion* on the line. Explain how you made your decision.

1. _____ Beethoven represents the highest level of musical genius.

2. _____ Like Bach and Mozart before him, he [Beethoven] came from a family of musicians.

3. _____ Beethoven jumped up from the piano, exclaiming, "I will not play for such swine!"

4. _____ Doctors could do nothing to halt the course of his physical and emotional torment.

5. _____ Works created after his emotional crisis have a new power and heroism.

6. _____ He played for Goethe [pronounced Ger-ta] and the two artists walked and talked together.

7. _____ His Sixth Symphony, the "Pastoral," beautifully expresses his recollections of life in the country.

8. _____ Friends had to communicate with him through an ear trumpet, and during his last eight years he carried notebooks in which people would write questions and comments.

Finding Information to Support Conclusions

The conclusions listed below are from the reading selection. Find information to support each conclusion. Check whether the supporting sentences are facts or opinions. When it is not clear whether the sentence is a fact or an opinion, check *Not Sure.*

	Fact	Opinion	Not Sure
Conclusion 1: Beethoven had to take on adult responsibilities at a young age. Information: *He became legal guardian of his brothers.*	✓		
Conclusion 2: He was a perfectionist. Information: _____			
Conclusion 3: He had a "hot temper." Information: _____			

Understanding Metaphor

A metaphor is an indirect comparison between two seemingly unlike things. For example, light is being compared to a knife in "The light *stabs at* the darkness." A tree is being compared to a guard in "The giant tree *stood watch over* the house and the people living there." Study the fairly common metaphors italicized in the excerpts below. Then decide what two things are being compared in each case. Discuss each metaphor with your classmates.

1. But when he learned that Napoleon had proclaimed himself emperor of the French, Beethoven "*flew into a rage* and cried out, 'He too is nothing but an ordinary man! . . .'"

2. " . . . 'Now he [Napoleon] will *trample under foot* all of the rights of man and only indulge his ambition. He will exalt himself above all others and become a tyrant!'"

3. He carried music sketchbooks everywhere, jotting down new ideas, revising and refining old ones. These early notes often seem crude and uninspired when compared to their final versions, which were *hammered out* through great labor.

Discovering Differences in Musical Styles

1. Bring to class a record or tape of the kind of music you like best. Play it for some of your classmates. Explain what you enjoy about the music and ask for their reactions.

2. Listen to the Beethoven recording again. How does it compare to the music you brought to class? List the similarities and differences in the chart below. Consider things such as the mood (how the music makes you feel), the rhythm, the various instruments, and so forth.

Similarities	Differences

3. In the Western Hemisphere, Beethoven's music is considered classical. What makes "classical" music different from other kinds of music? Was the music you brought to class classical? Discuss your ideas with your classmates.

Ideas for Discussion and/or Writing

1. The selection presented in this unit leaves out some of the important details of Beethoven's life. For example, we are not told anything about the events leading to and surrounding his death. Using an encyclopedia or another reference, find information to add to what you have read here. Share your new insights with your classmates.

2. In the library find short biographical sketches of at least two other composers. Your teacher or a librarian may be able to help you locate sources. Do you see any similarities in their lives? How do their lives compare with that of Beethoven?

3. The author describes at least two paradoxes, or contradictions, in Beethoven's personality. Discuss the meaning of these apparent contradictions. Think of any similar paradoxes in your own life or in the life of someone you know well. Share them with a classmate.

▶ Orderly and methodical when composing, Beethoven dressed sloppily and lived in incredibly messy apartments.

▶ He claimed the highest moral principles, but he was often unscrupulous in dealing with publishers.

4. Using the biographical sketch of Beethoven as an example, write a summary of your own life. Include not only the main events but also the details surrounding them. Tell more than just the facts. Include opinions and feelings. In addition, include any paradoxes that you may have noticed. Share your sketch with a classmate. Ask the following questions: What new things have you learned about me? Is there anything in my summary that is not clear to you? Can you think of ways it might be improved?

Notes

1. William Shakespeare was a seventeenth-century English dramatist and poet. Some say he was the world's greatest writer.

2. Michelangelo Buonarroti was a renowned sixteenth-century Italian artist.

3. Johann Sebastian Bach was a famous German composer of the eighteenth century.

4. Wolfgang Amadeus Mozart was a famous Austrian composer of the eighteenth century.

5. Franz Joseph Haydn was a famous eighteenth-century Austrian composer.

Unit 4 / Business

THE IMPACT OF COMPUTERS ON PEOPLE

Numerous software packages are available to simplify the work of engineers.

While many people know something about computers, not all have had direct experience with them. Have you had direct experience using a computer? If so, for what purposes did you use it? As a tool, what advantages did it have for you? In what ways do you think computers have changed the societies in which they have been introduced?

Read the following statements. Check the ones you think are true.

a. Computers can only *benefit* the societies in which they are found.

b. Prices paid for many products are lower than they would be if there were no computers.

c. The Constitution of the United States guarantees its citizens the right to privacy.

d. One thing a computer cannot do is paint pictures.

e. Because computers are so advanced, people can be safe in assuming that the information stored in them is accurate.

Computers have freed their users from many of the dull tasks that have, in the past, kept them slaves to detail. In addition, computers have made it possible for people to do things they could only dream about before. However, behind their tremendous advantages lurk dangers that could ruin lives and reputations if computer usage is not controlled.

The IMPACT of COMPUTERS on PEOPLE

Donald H. Sanders

The computer is one of the most powerful forces in society today. It's being put to use everywhere, it seems—in homes and in organizations of all sizes—and no one can doubt that this usage is having a strong impact on many people. But the computer is the driving force behind an information revolution, and as in any revolution some innocent people may be harmed. Let's look briefly here at some of the positive and negative effects that computer usage may have on people.

THE POSITIVE IMPACT

Many people enjoy challenging careers in computer departments as managers, systems designers, programmers, and operators. But we all benefit from computer usage. We benefit *on the job* even though we aren't computer specialists. We benefit as *consumers* of the goods and services provided by computer-using organizations. And we benefit *at home* by using personal computers for work and for play.

Employment Benefits

Each day, computers help millions of people do their jobs more effectively. For example, they can help *managers* decide on a future course of action (the planning function), and they can then help with the follow-up checks on performance to see if planned goals are being achieved

---

Definitions and Clues

systems designers: People who draw up plans for equipment and programs for computers.

programmers: People who set up the instructions that the computer follows.

(the control function). By using accurate and timely facts supplied by data base management software, a manager can do a better job of identifying problems and opportunities. The facts retrieved by such software can then be manipulated by a spreadsheet package to help the manager plan alternate courses of action. And managers may not need to spend as much time in controlling when a computer can respond with a triggered report if actual performance varies from what was planned. The time saved in controlling may allow managers to give more attention to employee concerns, and this, in turn, may result in improved morale.

But employment benefits certainly aren't restricted to managers. *Healthcare researchers and other scientists* now use computers to conduct research into complex problem areas that couldn't otherwise be studied. *Lawyers* use online legal data banks to locate precedent cases in order to serve clients better. *Salespeople* can receive more timely information about products in stock, can promise customers that their sales orders will be handled promptly, and can thus improve their sales performance because of computer systems. And the job duties of some *office* and *factory workers* have changed from routine, repetitive operations to more varied and appealing tasks through computer usage. For example, office workers who understand text processing, computing, and data communications usually have vital roles and are given crucial office functions to perform.

Benefits Received from Computer-Using Organizations

People also benefit as the *consumers* of the goods and services provided by computer-using organizations. Here are some examples:

▶ *Greater efficiency.* Because businesses have avoided waste and have improved efficiency through the use of computers, the prices we now pay are less than they would otherwise have been. For example, about one-third of all the dairy cows in the nation are now bred, fed, milked, and monitored for productivity with the help of computers. With only half as many cows, the dairy industry today produces all the milk that was supplied 15 years ago. Computer uses like this can significantly improve productivity—the amount of goods or services that people and machines (and cows) can produce from a given amount of input. And such productivity gains usually lead to higher levels of real income for more people.

Definitions and Clues

data: In this case, information that can be processed by the computer.

software: The information fed to the computer so that it can do its job (as opposed to hardware, which refers to the equipment itself).

online: A kind of data bank giving back information without delay.

precedent: Coming before (*pre-* means before; *-ced-* means to go).

text processing: Using programs that make it possible to store words, paragraphs, and so forth.

monitored: Checked (*mon-* refers to a warning).

▶ *Better service.* People may now receive better service from *government agencies.* In contrast to the bureaucratic runaround that often accompanies a call to city hall, a Long Beach, California, system allows citizens to dial a single number, get the right city department, and be guaranteed a response. The computer creates a record of each call, prints a letter to the caller, and sends a copy to the appropriate city council member. If a final disposition on a call isn't received within a given time, a follow-up procedure is triggered. The service benefits people receive from *business* computers include (1) shorter waiting lines at banks, airline ticket offices, and hotel and car-rental desks, (2) faster and more accurate answers to the inquiries of people served by the businesses, and (3) more efficient customer service and control of inventory in retail outlets. And the service benefits people receive from computers in *health care* include (1) faster and more thorough testing to detect and identify disease, (2) more accurate methods of physiological monitoring, and (3) better control of lab test results and the dispensing of drugs.

Benefits from Personal Computing

▶ *Entertainment and hobby benefits.* A personal computer (pc) can entertain you with hundreds of challenging games. And pc users can compose music, "paint" pictures, store and maintain stamp and coin collection records, and polish their foreign language skills.

▶ *Educational benefits.* Programs can be educational as well as entertaining. Educators agree that the home pc can be a powerful motivating and learning tool. Thousands of educational programs are available in such categories as reading, languages, science, mathematics, social studies, and art and music. The National Education Association reviews educational programs and puts its "teacher certified" NEA seal on those that meet its standards. When children (and adults) use a pc, they have some control over what they learn, how they learn, and how fast they learn. Making a sophisticated machine do one's bidding is fun for many people.

▶ *Personal finance benefits.* A pc can help you budget and balance your checkbook, control your installment purchases, control your home's energy use, and analyze your investments. If you want information on current stock prices, you can call a toll-free number,

---

Definitions and Clues

bureaucratic: Related to a complex government organization consisting mainly of nonelected officials.

disposition: In this case, a concluding report.

inventory: To make a list of everything in stock (*inven-* means to come upon).

physiological: Referring to body functions (*physio-* refers to the body). The first part of the sentence is a clue.

do one's bidding: Be prepared to do what someone asks you to do.

installment: Paid for a little at a time in fixed payments (*install-* refers to a fixed position).

stock: In this case, a share that a company sells to people who want ownership rights.

gain access to the data base of Dow Jones & Company,[1] and use programs to obtain information on any stock listed on any of the six major exchanges in the United States.

THE POTENTIAL DANGERS

In spite of the many benefits we gain from computer usage, such usage also has potential dangers and problems.

Employment Problems

. . . Some managers whose decisions were structured and repetitive found that programs could be written to take over many of their duties. Fewer managers were then needed to perform the remaining job functions. During the first half of the 1980s, middle-management ranks were reduced in many large firms. Clerical employees have often been displaced by computers too. And a significant displacement problem is accompanying the increased use of computer-controlled robots in production operations . . .

Data Gathering Problems

A staggering volume of personal information has been gathered by government agencies and private organizations. The federal government alone maintains over 4,500 data systems containing over 3.4 *billion* records and dossiers on people. And there are hundreds of private firms such as credit bureaus that collect and then sell personal information. Among the problems associated with all this data gathering are:

▶ *Gathering data without a valid need to know.* One example of questionable data gathering involves the firms that collect personal data about people for insurance companies, employers, and credit grantors. These data about a person may be obtained by an interviewer from two or three of the person's neighbors or acquaintances. In 10 or 20 minutes, the interviewer may ask questions about the subject's use of alcohol or drugs, whether there's anything adverse about his or her reputation or lifestyle, and if there's any news of domestic troubles or reports of dubious business practices. Questions calling for detailed responses on such matters in such a short time are an open invitation to gossip, opinionated answers, and faulty moral assessments. But this data gathering method has been used by a large consumer reporting service. Once stored in a computer data bank, the contents of a person's file are available to system users for a small fee.

Definitions and Clues

exchanges: A stock exchange is a place where stocks are bought and sold.

dossiers: A group of papers about a specific subject or person; a file.

credit bureaus: Agencies that file and distribute the payment records of people buying on credit.

adverse: Against.

dubious: Doubtful.

assessments: In this case, judgments.

▶ *Gathering inaccurate and incomplete data.* Another data gathering problem is caused by unintentional mistakes made in filling out input forms and keying records. There may be fewer people to catch errors in a computer-based system—and the speed with which inaccurate information is made available to system users may be much faster than the speed with which errors are found and corrected. For example, in converting data on a questionnaire into machine-readable form, a data entry operator may hit the 1 key instead of the 2 key (where 1 is the code for "yes" and 2 is the code for "no") on a question concerning a felony conviction, a prior bankruptcy, or a history of mental disorder or venereal disease. You can appreciate the possible consequences of this unintentional mistake! Finally, records are also subject to serious errors of omission. If, for example, an individual is arrested and accused of auto theft, this fact will likely be entered into several law enforcement data banks. But if the person is found innocent of charges, this very important fact that's needed to complete the record may *not* be entered into the data banks . . .

The Privacy Issue

Every person has a right to privacy—a legitimate right to limit access to personal and often sensitive information. If a law enforcement data bank permits the arrest of an innocent person and then results in the creation of an arrest record that may not be purged from the system, and if a lack of systems security subsequently permits the circulation of this arrest record to prospective employers and credit agencies, these deficiencies have certainly contributed to an invasion of the individual's privacy.

We've been discussing an individual's "right" to privacy, but this isn't a right that's spelled out in the Constitution.[2] And what one person may consider to be a privacy right may be judged by others to be an item of public concern. For example, if a newspaper reporter learns that a member of Congress has placed unqualified relatives on the government payroll and if the reporter then reveals this fact and prints the names and salaries of the relatives, she has undoubtedly infringed on their privacy. But she has also used rights guaranteed to her in the Bill of Rights[3] (the First Amendment's freedom of speech and freedom of the press) to perform a public service. Thus, there are legitimate rights operating against privacy in some cases. In short, since privacy isn't a specific constitutional right, and since a balance has to be struck between the personal need for privacy and society's need for legitimate information, *the extent to which individuals are given privacy protection must depend on judicial and legislative decisions.* That is, the *continuous task* of balancing human rights against basic freedoms in order to establish privacy controls is the responsibility of the judicial and legislative branches of government.

Definitions and Clues

keying: Typing in data on a computer keyboard.

felony: A serious crime.

venereal: Referring to the sex organs (*vener-* refers to love).

legitimate: Lawful (*ligiti-* refers to law). "Right to privacy" is a clue.

prospective: Looked forward to (*pro-* means forward; *-spect-* means to look).

judicial: Relating to the part of government responsible for deciding what the laws mean.

legislative: Relating to the part of government responsible for making the laws.

Checking Your Prereading Reactions

Return to the statements on page 29. Look again at your reactions. Discuss whether your ideas have changed after reading "The Impact of Computers on People."

Understanding Intended Meaning

Work with a classmate to complete the following tasks.

1. According to the author, five groups of people benefit from computers on the job. List the five groups and briefly write how each group benefits.

2. List a few benefits consumers can receive from business computers.

3. Write some specific examples of how a personal computer (pc) can be used in the areas of entertainment, education, and finance.

4. Describe in your own words what the author feels are some of the dangers of computers.

Making Inferences

Discuss the following questions with your class.

1. What do you think the author means by an "information revolution"? (See page 30.)

2. Pretend that you are gathering information about a particular individual for a consumer reporting service. You have decided to interview the neighbors of the person in question, thinking that they will be able to give you valuable information. What would be the author's reaction to your decision?

3. In what ways might the gathering of inaccurate or incomplete data (see page 34) be disastrous for individuals in the following situations?

    ▶ applying for a job
    ▶ applying for a loan to buy a house

4. What two freedoms in the Bill of Rights are mentioned in this reading? In what ways are they in the best interest of United States citizens? What dangers do they pose?

5. The author claims that the " . . . task of balancing human rights against basic freedoms in order to establish privacy controls is the responsibility of the judicial and legislative branches of government" (page 34). What kinds of tasks might he have in mind for each branch concerning the issue of privacy versus the public's right to know? The definitions in the "Definitions and Clues" on page 34 may be of help.

Being Aware of Organization

In an introduction to a reading, authors often suggest how the reading will be organized.

Reread the first paragraph of the selection. Based on the information given there, write the main topic or subjects you expect to be covered.

_____

_____

Knowing the overall organization of a selection can frequently aid in recalling important information. Quickly review the entire reading. Then complete the outline below.

Note: It is not important that the information be listed in the exact order in which it is presented. It is important, however, that you place items in the appropriate categories.

Topic: THE IMPACT OF COMPUTERS ON PEOPLE

I. The positive impact

   A. Employment benefits

      1. Benefits to managers

      2. _____

      3. _____

      4. _____

      5. _____

   B. Benefits received from computer-using organizations

      1. Greater efficiency

      2. _____

         a. Government agencies

         b. _____

         c. _____

   C. _____

      1. _____

      2. _____

      3. _____

II. The potential dangers

A. _____

B. _____

    1. Gathering data without a valid need to know

    2. _____

C. The privacy issue

Ideas for Discussion and/or Writing

1. If you had a robot in your home, what duties would you program it to perform? Let your imagination be your guide. Share your ideas with your classmates.

2. Imagine you are the manager of a large office and you know that computers are going to take over the jobs of 20 percent of your staff before the end of the year. Because you do not want the news to destroy the good morale your staff has developed over the years, come to some decisions about how to handle the problem. Give what you consider to be valid reasons for your decisions. Compare your decisions with those of a classmate. Are there any that you would change?

3. Look up the United States' Bill of Rights in the library. What other freedoms are included other than freedoms of speech and of the press? If you had to choose only one "right" of which you could be guaranteed, which one would you choose? Develop arguments defending your choice.

4. Over the years much controversy has surrounded the issue of privacy versus the public's right to know. In the library find out as much information as you can about this issue. Using an outline form similar to that on pages 36–37, organize your findings. Use the information to prepare for one of the following:

▶ a group discussion
▶ a debate
▶ a composition.

5. Pretend it is the year 2020. Describe what you think life will be like because of advances made in computers. Your description can be accomplished through several different means:

▶ a science-fiction story or drama to be acted out
▶ a magazine article predicting the future
▶ an original cartoon
▶ words to a song.

Perhaps you can think of other ideas. Discuss them with your teacher and at least one other classmate before beginning the project.

Notes

1. *Dow Jones and Company:* The New York firm that publishes the Dow Jones Index, a listing of the various price levels of groups of stocks and bonds.

2. *The [United States] Constitution:* The formal principles set up in 1787 upon which the United States government is based.

3. *Bill of Rights:* The first ten amendments to the Constitution of the United States.

Unit 5 / Natural Science

SURVIVAL IN THE WILD: THE PREDATOR AND THE PREY

You might not consider human behavior to be in any way like the behavior of a predator hunting prey. But consider these questions: Have you ever tried to catch a frog or a butterfly? If so, you were probably trying to catch it using strategies similar to those of a predator hunting prey. What kinds of movements did you make to capture it? What did it do to get away? Who won in the struggle?

Read the following statements. Check the ones you think are true.

a. There are organisms (living things) that spend their entire lives living and feeding on the bodies of others.

b. An organism's colors can serve as a defense against predators.

c. Some organisms "pretend" to be poisonous to keep from being eaten by predators.

d. Predators are a nuisance because they ruin the lives of their prey and sometimes cause horrible suffering.

Using Marginal Glossing as a Study Aid

Look at the notes written in the margins at the beginning of the reading selection on page 41. These notes provide a study aid known as "marginal glossing." It is a technique whereby the reader restates or paraphrases what has been said. It is similar to finding a main idea in a reading selection (see pages 6 and 15). However, in this case, you are looking for the main idea of a smaller segment of text. In addition, marginal glossing often includes a simplification of complex ideas rephrased in the reader's own words.

Complete the marginal glossing for the rest of the reading.

In order for organisms to exist, they must work with the other organisms and elements in the environment to achieve and maintain a delicate balance. The following reading selection describes how entire populations of organisms adapt to and affect the world around them. You may be in for some surprises.

Survival in the Wild: The Predator and the Prey

CECIE STARR
AND RALPH TAGGART

●

PREDATION

On "Predator" Versus "Parasite"

Of all community interactions, predation is perhaps the most riveting of our attention (as well as the prey's). Dramatic examples abound, including the confrontation between the leopard and the baboon shown on page 39. A goat pulling up a thistle plant for breakfast, although less dramatic, is no less a case of predation—the prey is a living organism killed by the predator. But what about grasshoppers or horses, which graze on plants without killing them; or mosquitoes, which take blood from your arm and then fly off? What about ticks and fleas, which live on the host and take blood for long periods but get off to lay their eggs elsewhere? What about internal parasites such as tapeworms, external ones such as lice, or the parasitic plants called mistletoe, which spend their entire lives with the host?

The terminology available for these diverse interactions is ex-

Many *very* different events can be considered examples of a predator/prey relationship.

Definitions and Clues

riveting: In this case, capable of holding.

abound: Being great in number.

thistle: A prickly weed.

terminology: Technical terms appropriate to a specific field of study. Also known sometimes as jargon.

diverse: Unlike the others (*di-* refers to aside; *-ver-* refers to turning).

tensive and sometimes contradictory. Predators get their food from other living organisms (their *prey*), but they do not live on or in the prey and may or may not kill it. Parasites also get their food from other living organisms (their *hosts*), but they live on or in the host for a good part of their life cycle and may or may not kill it.

Stable coexistence for both populations is likely when predation keeps the prey population in check (it prevents the prey population from overshooting its carrying capacity). Predators can do this when they reproduce quickly relative to the prey and are capable of eating more when there are more prey organisms around.

Oscillations are likely when predators reproduce more slowly than their prey, when they eat only so many prey organisms at a time regardless of how many are around, and when the carrying capacity of the environment is high for their prey.

An idealized cyclic oscillation of predator and prey abundance appears in Figure 1. The cycling is caused by time lags in the predator's response to changes in the abundance of prey. (A "time lag" is an interval of time between two related events.)

A predator gets its food from another living organism. The predator may *or* may not kill the organism in the process. However, it does *not* live in the organism. Only parasites do that. Note: "Prey" are organisms that provide food for predators. "Hosts" are organisms that provide food for parasites.

"Stable coexistence" happens when predator and prey keep each other's population in balance. If their populations are not in balance, "oscillations" can result.

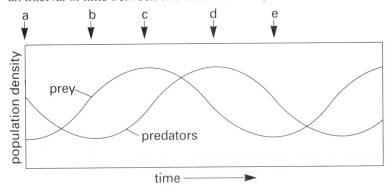

Figure 1.   Idealized cycles of predator and prey abundance. The cycling is caused by time lags in the predator's response to changes in prey abundance. Starting at time *a*, the prey population is at a low density, so the predator population is hungry and declining. The prey population responds to the decline by increasing, but the predators continue to decline for a while until increased predator reproduction gets under way (time *b*).

Both populations increase until the increasing predation halts further growth of the prey population (time lag) and it begins to decline. The prey suffer further impact from predation as the predators continue their increase, which slows as they feel the effects of starvation from lower prey density (time *d*). At time (*e*), we are back where we started and a new cycle begins.

Definitions and Clues

oscillation: Swinging back and forth.

cyclic: Involving events that repeat themselves (*cycl-* refers to circle). See the sentence following in the reading.

Time lags certainly contribute to the lynx-hare cycles. When prey population density is at its peak, predators are not usually numerous enough to bring about an immediate decline of the huge hordes of hares. It takes time for the lynx population to increase by way of reproduction and by migration of lynx into areas where prey are abundant. More abundant food can promote survival, more rapid development, even fertility, but there is a lag time between the birth of potential predators and the point at which they are mature enough to take prey.

In this example, increased predation can make a major contribution to the decline of the prey population, but it probably cannot trigger the decline. What does?

There is some evidence that recurring wildfires, floods, and insect outbreaks have indirect bearing on the hare-lynx cycle. Such environmental disturbances can destroy mature forest canopies that thereby create favorable conditions for different plant species that are adapted to moving in and becoming established in exposed settings. These species flourish until the species typical of the mature forest system become reestablished and gradually succeed them, in ways that will be described shortly.

Now, the so-called early successional species provide ideal forage for the hares; in fact, the peaks in hare population densities correspond to the occurrence of this type of vegetation cover. However, the early successional shrubs and trees include alders, poplar, black spruce, and birch species—all of which produce toxins in especially high concentrations in new shoots. During winter, the hares prefer to feed on other plant parts and suffer no ill effects. When population density is high, though, the hares destroy the harmless parts of their winter forage, and they are forced to begin feeding on the toxic shoots. Experiments show that hares ingesting high concentrations of the plant toxins rapidly lose weight and become severely stressed.

Thus the cyclic fluctuations in population density may be a consequence of hares preying on plants and are simply amplified by lynx preying on hares. The built-in chemical defenses of certain plants prevent even more devastating increases in the numbers of hares.

Definitions and Clues

lynx: A wild cat with thick fur and a short tail; found on the North American continent.

hare: An animal similar to a rabbit but with larger feet and longer legs.

hordes: Large groups.

canopies: High protective coverings serving as a "roof" of sorts.

forage: Food found by searching around.

toxins: Poisonous (*tox-* means poison).

ingesting: Taking in.

PREY DEFENSES

When you stop to think about it, the fact that the plants described above defend themselves against being eaten by snowshoe hares is rather remarkable. How do such defenses arise? From what is known about evolutionary processes, it is clear that predators and prey exert continual selection pressure on each other. When some new, heritable means of defense spreads through the prey population, only the predators equipped to counter the defense of their prey survive to reproduce. Thus, when the prey evolves, the predator also evolves to some extent because the change affects selection pressures operating between the predator and prey. Again, this type of joint evolution of two (or more) species that are interacting in close ecological fashion is called coevolution. Let's take a look at some of the outcomes of predator-prey interactions.

Camouflage

One evolutionary outcome of predation is the capacity of many species of prey (and of predators) to "hide" in the open. Camouflage is an adaptation in form, patterning, color, or behavior that enables an organism to blend with its surroundings, the better to escape detection.

For example, a desert plant (*Lithops*) resembles small rocks in shape and color. Only during the brief rainy season, when other vegetation and water are more plentiful for herbivores, do these "living rocks" put forth brightly colored flowers and draw the attention of pollinators. (Camouflage, of course, is not the exclusive domain of prey. Predators that rely on stealth also blend well with the background. Think about polar bears against snow, tigers against tall-stalked and golden grasses, and pastel spiders against pastel flower petals.)

Definitions and Clues

evolutionary: Referring to evolution, a process by which species change over time to better fit their environment (*evolut-* refers to rolling out).

heritable: Capable of being passed from parent to offspring.

ecological: Relating to ecology, the study of organisms and their relationship to the environment.

herbivores: Organisms that feed on plants (an herb is a type of plant).

pollinators: Organisms that transfer pollen (the male element) from one part of a plant to another to cause fertilization.

stealth: Movement that is sneaky so as not to be noticed.

Moment-of-Truth Defenses

When cornered, some prey species defend themselves with display behavior that may startle or intimidate a predator. Such behavior can create momentary confusion, and a moment may be all it takes for the prey to escape. When attacked, the bombardier beetle raises its abdomen and sprays a noxious chemical at its predator. (It is an effective adaptation in some cases, but grasshopper mice have a behavioral counteradaptation. These mice pick up the beetle, shove its tail end into the earth, and munch the head end.)

The bombardier beetle is one of many animals as well as plant species that release chemicals to repel or otherwise deter a potential attacker. Chemicals serve as warning odors, repellants, alarm substances, and outright poisons. Earwigs, grasshoppers, and skunks can produce awful odors. The foliage and seeds of some plants contain tannins, which taste bitter and which decrease the digestibility of the plant material; the tissues of other plants incorporate terpenes, which can be toxic. Nibbling on a buttercup (*Ranunculus*) leads to highly irritated mucous membranes in the mouth.

Warning Coloration and Mimicry

One consequence of predation is the existence of many prey species that are bad-tasting, toxic, or able to sting or otherwise inflict pain on their attackers. Often, toxic prey species are decked out with conspicuous colors and bold patterns that serve warning to potential predators. Inexperienced predators might attack a black-and-white striped skunk, a bright orange monarch butterfly, or a yellow-banded wasp. As a result of the experience, they quickly learn to associate the colors and patterning with pain or digestive upsets.

Other prey species *not* equipped with such defenses can still sport warning colors or patterns that *resemble* those of distasteful, toxic, or dangerous species. The resemblance of an edible species to a relatively inedible one is a form of mimicry.

Definitions and Clues

noxious: Harmful (*nox-* refers to injury).

deter: To stop (*de-* means away from). See also "repel" in the same sentence.

foliage: Leaves.

tannins: Strong substances used to make leather.

terpenes: An element found in the oils of some plants.

mucous membranes: The wet linings of all body channels that interact with the air.

decked out: Dressed for display.

Some mimics are as unpalatable as their models; they are called *Müllerian mimics* (after Fritz Müller,[1] who named the phenomenon). Others may be quite edible yet are still avoided; they are called *Batesian mimics* (after Henry Bates,[2] who discovered this class of mimics).

There are other types of mimicry. In *aggressive mimicry,* parasites or predators bear resemblances to their hosts or prey. In *speed mimicry,* sluggish, easy-to-catch prey species resemble fast-running or fast-flying species that predators have given up trying to catch. (This might well be termed "frustration" mimicry.)

Definitions and Clues

unpalatable: Not acceptable to the taste.

Checking Your Prereading Reactions

Return to the statements on page 40. Look again at your reactions. Discuss whether your ideas have changed after reading "Survival in the Wild: The Predator and the Prey."

Understanding Intended Meaning

Discuss the following questions with your class.

1.   How are a predator and a parasite alike?

2.   How are they different?

3.   Is a predator or a parasite involved in the situations below? Check the appropriate column and discuss your answers.

		Predator	Parasite
1.	a flea on your dog		
2.	a bird eating an insect		
3.	a cow grazing on the grass		
4.	a tick in your cat's fur		

	Predator	Parasite
5. a vampire bat feeding on the blood of a cow		
6. a tapeworm in a monkey		
7. an otter swallowing a fish		
8. a leopard feeding off a baboon		
9. lice in a child's hair		

4. How do time lags make cyclic oscillation between predator and prey a possibility?

5. Increased predation can cause a decline in prey population. In the case of the lynx/hare cycle, what other kinds of events or conditions can cause this decline?

6. Explain how predators and prey can exert continual selection pressure on each other (see page 42). What is this process called? Reread the remainder of the reading selection and find examples of this process.

7. How can camouflage work for both predators and prey?

8. From the context, how would you define mimicry? What types of mimicry have been identified? How do they differ from one another?

Using Marginal Glossing to Write a Summary

Reread your marginal glossing. Use it to write a brief summary of the reading. Compare your summary with that of a classmate and make any changes that seem appropriate.

Looking at Cause and Effect

Work with a small group to complete the following tasks.

1. Suppose hares began to reproduce more slowly than lynx. Describe what would happen.

2. Look again at the reading and make a list of all of the effects of predation you can find.

Interpreting a Graph

Study the graph on page 42. Then answer the following questions.

1. Consider points *a* and *b* on the graph. Which of these points represents the greater relative abundance of predators to prey?

2. Answer the same question for points *c* and *d*.

3. Can you find a point on the graph at which conditions are about the same as point *b*? Label it on the graph as point *f*.

4. Was the graph helpful? If so, in what way?

Improving the Ability to Extrapolate

To extrapolate means to extend knowledge to other situations. Although it does not appear to be the intention of the authors to include humankind in a discussion of predator/prey or parasite/host relationships, you may find such a discussion of interest. Consider, for example, the following questions and discuss each one in small groups. Have one person in your group take notes. Have your group share its conclusions with the rest of the class.

1. Can you think of ways in which humans might be considered predators?

2. How might humans be considered prey?

3. What defenses might humans use as prey?

4. Are there any circumstances in which humans might be similar to parasites? Consider human relationships.

5. In what way might a person play the role of the host in a parasite/host relationship?

6. What defenses does a potential host need to develop in order to prevent being used in this manner?

Ideas for Discussion and/or Writing

1. In the library find aditional examples of the following kinds of defenses used in the wild: camouflage, moment-of-truth, warning coloration, and mimicry. Ask your teacher, the librarian, or a classmate to help you in your search.

2. Find books or short stories in which humans are, in a physical sense, prey to other humans. Read a few of them. Compare the situations found in each and the strategies used by both prey and predator. Below are some examples:

The Pearl (book) by John Steinbeck

"The Most Dangerous Game" (story) by Richard Connell

"The Sniper" (story) by Liam O'Flaherty

"Flight" (story) by John Steinbeck

3. In small groups create a short scene in which humans employ psychological defenses. These defenses might include reactions such as ignoring a verbal insult or using logical arguments to block an attempt by one person to make a host of another. Act out your scene. Once your group has practiced the scene several times, you may want to present it to the rest of the class.

Notes

1. Fritz Müller was a nineteenth-century German naturalist.

2. Henry Bates was a nineteenth-century British naturalist.

Unit 6 / History

IMMIGRANTS TO THE UNITED STATES DURING THE NINETEENTH CENTURY: THE IRISH AND THE GERMANS

WANTED

A Cook or Chambermaid. They must be American, Scotch, Swiss, or Africans— no Irish.

Newspaper advertisement from the *New York Evening Post,* September 4, 1830.

In recent years, many nations have experienced an influx of newcomers from other lands. Some of these newcomers have been classified as immigrants, others as refugees. How do immigrants differ from refugees? What different problems do you think they might face? For what reasons are immigrants and refugees now coming to the United States and going to other countries throughout the world?

Have you recently moved to a new country with a different culture or are you planning to move? What were your reasons for this move? What kinds of personal choices were involved or will be involved?

Large numbers of Irish and German immigrants came to the United States during the nineteenth century. The purpose of the following activity is to see what you already know about their circumstances. Check the group being described in each statement. If you are not sure, take a guess.

	Statement	Irish	Germans
1.	The majority were in danger of starving if they remained in their homeland.		
2.	Many were able to leave their homeland with a small amount of money.		
3.	Because they were mainly Catholics, they were often resented by United States citizens.		
4.	Most came to the United States for economic reasons.		

Using Marginal Glossing as a Study Aid

In Unit 5 you learned that marginal glossing is a study aid. You learned that it involves a restatement or a paraphrase of the main ideas in the text. In the margin beside each paragraph in the reading selection, restate or paraphrase the main ideas.

The nineteenth-century immigrants to the United States came seeking a better life. Many came to escape great suffering because of natural causes or because of systems that kept them in poverty. But what many of them found in their new land was not exactly what they expected.

Immigrants to the United States During the Nineteenth Century:

The Irish and the Germans

ROBERT DIVINE, T. H. BREEN, GEORGE FREDRICKSON, AND R. HAL WILLIAMS

★ ★ ★ ★ ★ ★ ★ ★ ★ ★ ★ ★ ★ ★ ★ ★ ★ ★ ★

Between 1820 and 1840, an estimated 700,000 immigrants arrived in the United States, mainly from the British Isles and German-speaking areas of continental Europe (see figure). During the 1840s this substantial flow suddenly became a flood. No less than 4,200,000 crossed the Atlantic between 1840 and 1860, and about 3 million of these arrived in the single decade between 1845 and 1855. This was the greatest influx in proportion to total population—then about 20 million—that the nation has ever experienced. The largest single source of the new mass immigration was Ireland, but Germany was not far behind. Smaller contingents came from Switzerland, Norway, Sweden, and the Netherlands.

Definitions and Clues

influx: A flowing in (*-flux* means to flow). See the previous sentence in the reading.

contingents: In this case, groups that represent others in the larger population.

Immigration to the United States, 1820–1860

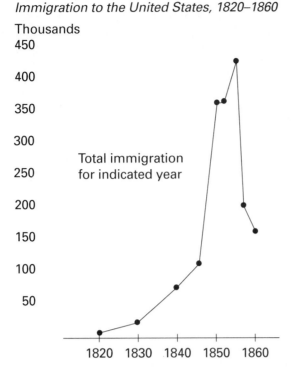

SOURCE: *Historical Statistics of the United States, Colonial Times to 1970, Bicentennial Edition* (Washington, D.C.: U.S. Bureau of the Census, 1975).

This massive transatlantic movement had many causes; some people were "pushed" out of their homes, while others were "pulled" toward America. The great "push" factor that caused a million and a half Irish to forsake the Emerald Isle between 1845 and 1854 was the great potato famine. Escape to America was made possible by the low fares then prevailing on sailing ships bound from England to North America. Ships involved in the timber trade carried their bulky cargoes from Boston or Halifax to Liverpool; as an alternative to returning to America partly in ballast, they packed Irish immigrants into their holds. The squalor and misery in these "steerage" accommodations were almost beyond belief.

Definitions and Clues

forsake: To give up.

Emerald Isle: Ireland (the color emerald is a brilliant green).

prevailing: Generally accepted as current (-*vail*- refers to strong).

ballast: Heavy material used to make a ship more stable.

Immobilized by poverty and a lack of the skills required for pioneering in the West,[1] most of them remained in the northeast. By the 1850s, they constituted a substantial portion of the total population of Boston, New York, Philadelphia, and many smaller cities of the New England and Middle Atlantic states. Forced to subsist on low-paid menial labor and crowded into festering urban slums, they were looked down upon by most native-born Americans. Their devotion to Catholicism aroused Protestant resentment and mob violence.

The million or so Germans who also came in the late 1840s and early '50s were somewhat more fortunate. Most of them were also peasants, but they fled hard times rather than outright catastrophe. Changes in German landholding patterns and the rise of a fluctuating market economy put pressure on small operators. Those whose mortgages were foreclosed—or who could no longer make the regular payments to landlords that were the price of emancipation from feudal obligations—frequently opted for immigration to America. Unlike the Irish, they often escaped with a small amount of capital with which to make a fresh start in the New World.

Many German immigrants were artisans and sought to ply their trades in cities like New York, St. Louis, Cincinnati, and Milwaukee—all of which became centers of German-American population. But a large portion of those with peasant backgrounds went back to the land. The possession of diversified agricultural skills and small amounts of capital enabled many Germans to become successful midwestern farmers. In general, they encountered less prejudice and discrimination than the Irish. For those who were Protestant, religious affinity with their American neighbors made for relative

---

Definitions and Clues

subsist: To live below standard; merely exist (*sub-* means below; *-sist* refers to causing to stand up).

menial: Characteristic of a servant (*meni-* refers to servant).

festering: Creating unpleasantness (*feste-* refers to an ulcer or a sore).

mortgages: Promises to give property to someone to whom you owe money in case you cannot make your payments.

foreclosed: The property that was promised was claimed because the debtor could not make the payments.

emancipation: Freeing from authority (*e-* means out of).

feudal: Relating to feudalism, a system in which land is held in exchange for service.

opted: Made a choice. Related to the word "option" (*op-* means to choose).

capital: Money.

artisans: Persons skilled in making an item to be sold.

ply: In this case, to practice.

affinity: Here it means similarity (*a-* refers to being near to; *-fin-* refers to border or ends).

(a) Baron Biesele, upon his arrival in America (in German): "Hey, fellow countryman, where can we find a German tavern?"
Countryman (in German): "Damme. Do you think I'm a no-good like you? I am an American."

(b) Baron Biesele, first week after arrival (in German to another recently arrived German): "Well, Marianel, how do you like it in America?"
Marianel (in German): "Oh, Baron, the language, the language. I'll never learn it in all my life."

(c) Baron Biesele, two weeks after arrival (in German): "Can you tell us—Hey, beautiful Marianel, isn't that you?"
Marianel (in English): "You are mistaken. I don't talk Dutch."

These lithographs from the *Fliegende Blatter* (Cincinnati, 1847) feature the antics of Baron Biesele, a popular cartoon character in the German prototype of this short-lived Cincinnati periodical of the same name.

tolerance. But even Germans who were Catholic normally escaped the virulent scorn heaped upon the Irish, perhaps because they did not carry the added burden of being members of an ethnic group Americans had learned to despise from their English ancestors and cousins.[2]

What attracted or "pulled" most of the Irish, German, and other European immigrants to America was the promise of economic opportunity. A minority, like some of the German revolutionaries of 1848, chose the United States because they admired its democratic political system. But most immigrants were more interested in the chance to make a decent living than in voting or running for office.

The arrival of large numbers of immigrants worsened the already serious problems of America's rapidly growing cities. The old "walking city" in which rich and poor lived in close proximity near the center of town was changing to a more segregated environment. The advent of railroads and horse-drawn streetcars enabled the affluent

Definitions and Clues

virulent: Full of hate (*virul-* refers to poison).

proximity: Nearness (*prox-* refers to near).

advent: The arrival (*ad-* means to; *-ven-* refers to coming).

affluent: At or moving toward the state of being wealthy (*a-* here refers to toward; *-fluen-* refers to flowing).

to move to the first American suburbs, while areas nearer commercial and industrial centers became the congested abode of newcomers from Europe. Emerging slums, such as the notorious "Five Points" district in New York City, were characterized by overcrowding, poverty, disease, and crime. Recognizing that these conditions created potential dangers for the entire urban population, middle-class reformers worked for the professionalization of police forces, introduction of sanitary water and sewage disposal systems, and the upgrading of housing standards. They made some progress in these endeavors in the period before the Civil War,[3] but the lot of the urban poor, mainly immigrants, was not dramatically improved. For most of them, urban life remained unsafe, unhealthy, and unpleasant.

THE NEW WORKING CLASS

A majority of the immigrants ended up as wage workers in factories, mines, and construction camps, or as casual day laborers doing the many unskilled tasks required by urban and commercial growth. By providing a vast pool of cheap labor, they fueled and accelerated the Industrial Revolution. During the 1850s factory production in Boston and other port cities previously devoted to commerce grew—mainly because thousands of recent Irish immigrants were willing to work for the kind of low wages that almost guaranteed large profits for entrepreneurs.

By 1860 industrial expansion and immigration had created a working class of men and women who seemed destined for a life of low-paid wage labor. This reality stood in contrast to America's self-image as a land of opportunity and upward mobility. Wage labor was popularly viewed as a temporary condition from which workers were supposed to extricate themselves by hard work and frugality. According to Abraham Lincoln,[4] speaking in 1850 of the North's "free labor" society, "there is no such thing as a free man being fatally fixed for life, in the condition of a hired laborer." This ideal still had some validity in rapidly developing regions of the western states, but it was mostly myth when applied to the increasingly foreign born industrial workers of the Northeast.

Definitions and Clues

abode: Home.

notorious: Widely known in an unfavorable sense (*notor-* refers to being known).

urban: Referring to a city (the opposite is "rural," which refers to the countryside).

entrepreneurs: People who undertake the responsibility of owning a business (*entrepren-* refers to undertaking).

extricate: To move out of a difficult situation (*ex-* in this case means out).

frugality: The state of being thrifty.

validity: The state of being well-grounded or supported (*val-* refers to being strong).

Checking Your Prereading Reactions

Return to the statements on page 51. Look again at your reactions. Discuss whether your ideas have changed after reading "Immigrants to the United States During the Nineteenth Century: The Irish and the Germans."

Understanding Intended Meaning

Work with a small group to complete the following tasks.

1. Explain the "pull" and "push" factors of United States immigration during the nineteenth century. Find one example of each factor in the reading.

2. Describe the conditions faced by the Irish before, during, and after their immigration to the United States.

3. Tell how the situation of the Germans differed from that of the Irish. Include the differences in their reasons for coming as well as the conditions faced once they arrived.

4. Decide which group experienced the most prejudice and discrimination. Explain.

5. Describe the impact that these immigrants had on the work force in the United States.

Using Marginal Glossing to Write a Summary

Reread your marginal glossing. Use it to write a brief summary of the reading. Compare your summary with that of a classmate and make any changes that seem appropriate.

Discovering Irony

Discuss the following with your class.

Irony occurs when events or conditions turn out to be the opposite of what was expected. We say that such turns of events or conditions are "ironical." What was ironical about what happened to many of the nineteenth-century immigrants in their new land?

Making Inferences

Discuss the following questions with your class.

1. Think about Abraham Lincoln's words " . . . there is no such thing as a free man being fatally fixed for life, in the condition of a hired laborer" (page 56). In what way was this a myth when applied to the foreign-born industrial worker of the Northeast in the 1800s? Do you think it is still a myth today?

2. Look at the cartoons on page 55. What attitude are the cartoon characters expressing toward their original language and culture? Why do you think they are behaving in this way?

Relating the Selection to Personal/Cultural Experience

Have you ever had experiences comparable to those of the Irish and the Germans? If so, discuss the following questions with a small group.

1.   How were your own experiences similar to and/or different from those of the Irish and Germans?

2.   What personal or cultural characteristics and events helped you and others from your country improve the quality of your lives?

3.   To what extent were you able to maintain your own language and cultural identity during this process?

4.   What problems might you still have to face and what can you do to overcome them?

5.   In what ways do you feel you and others from your culture have contributed to the shaping of the society in your new country?

Reading Critically

Consider what it's like to move to a new country with a culture different from your own. Do you think that the authors present enough information about the Irish and German immigrants to give you a feeling of what their experiences were like? If not, what kinds of information do you feel would strengthen this reading, if the information were available? Discuss these questions with a small group.

Interpreting a Graph

Look at the graph on page 53. Notice that less than 50,000 people (see the vertical column on the left) emigrated to the United States in 1820 (see the horizontal line across the bottom). Study the graph and answer the following questions.

1.   During which time period in the mid-1800s did the United States experience its greatest increase in the immigrant population?

2.   During which period did the United States experience its greatest decrease?

3.   Approximately how many emigrated to the United States at the peak of immigration?

4.   Was this graph helpful? If so, in what way?

Ideas for Discussion and/or Writing

1.   Are you learning English in a country where it is a dominant language? If so, write several questions to ask native speakers of English. Below are a few sample questions.

    ▶ What do you think it would be like to live permanently in a foreign country and not be able to speak the language?

▶ What problems might you have other than those related to language?

▶ What would you miss the most about your own country?

Interview several people outside your class. After each interview, write down what you can remember of the answers you received. Share a few of the more interesting answers with your class.

2.   In the library find descriptions of other immigrants in other situations. Compare their experiences to those of the Irish and Germans as described in this reading section. How were the experiences alike? How were they different?

3.   Look again at the answers you gave to the questions on page 58 about the graph. Note the years you gave showing the largest decrease in the number of people emigrating to the United States (Question 2). Using other sources available in the library, explain what was happening in the United States at that time that may have been an influential factor.

4.   Pretend you are a scholar writing a history book. Write a brief account of the movement of immigrants to a new country from 1975 to the present. You may need library resources (books, journals, and newspapers) to aid you.

Notes

1.   In the United States at that time, large numbers of people called "pioneers" were moving from the East to the West to seek new opportunities.

2.   The English have had long-standing disputes with the Irish over the centuries. The hatred that developed is still felt today.

3.   The Civil War was fought between the Union (the northern states) and the Confederacy (the southern states) between the years 1861 and 1865.

4.   Abraham Lincoln was the sixteenth President of the United States. He served from 1861 to 1865, when he was assassinated. He is generally associated with the freeing of the slaves, a result of the Civil War.

Unit 7 / Literature

AN OCCURRENCE AT OWL CREEK BRIDGE

This story takes place during the Civil War, which was fought in the United States between 1861 and 1865. At that time, the country was divided into two parts: the North (represented by the Union army) and the South (represented by the Confederate army). The North eventually won the war. One of the results of the victory was the freeing of the black slaves in the South.

How would you define a "civil" war? How does it differ from other kinds of war? Can you think of other examples of civil wars? What problems were involved? Who won? What changes did the fighting bring about?

For many people, death is a difficult concept to deal with. If someone told you that you might not live much longer, what would your first thoughts be? How would you spend your remaining time? Consider the people you would want to see and the things you would want to do.

♦

Often, when facing death, people think of the things that have brought the most happiness to their lives, the everyday things that they would dearly miss. To a condemned man, some of life's treasures may take on even more significance. Read the following story to find out just how important such treasures can be.

An Occurrence at
Owl Creek Bridge

AMBROSE BIERCE[1]

I

A man stood upon a railroad bridge in northern Alabama, looking down into the swift water twenty feet below. The man's hands were behind his back, the wrists bound with a cord. A rope closely encircled his neck . . . Some loose boards supplied a footing for him and his executioners—two private soldiers of the Federal army,[2] directed by a sergeant . . . At a short remove upon the same temporary platform was an officer in the uniform of his rank, armed. He was a captain. A sentinel at each end of the bridge stood with his rifle . . .

The man who was engaged in being hanged was apparently about thirty-five years of age. He was a civilian . . . His features were good—a straight nose, firm mouth, broad forehead, from which his long, dark hair was combed straight back, falling behind his ears to the collar of his well-fitting frock coat. He wore a mustache and pointed beard, but no whiskers; his eyes were large and dark gray, and had a kindly expression . . .

The preparations being complete, the two private soldiers stepped aside and each drew away the plank upon which he had been standing . . . These movements left the condemned man and the sergeant standing on the two ends of the same plank . . . His face had not been covered nor his eyes bandaged. He looked a moment at his "unsteadfast footing," then let his gaze wander to the swirling water of the stream racing madly beneath his feet. A piece of dancing driftwood caught his attention and his eyes followed it down the current. How slowly it appeared to move! What a sluggish stream!

Definitions and Clues

executioners: Officials who kill someone who is thought to have committed a crime.

sentinel: One who watches or guards (*senti-* refers to watching).

civilian: In this case, relating to ordinary citizens, those not in the armed forces (*civi-* refers to citizen).

frock: A light coat worn over other clothing.

gaze: Stare.

He closed his eyes in order to fix his last thoughts upon his wife and children. The water, touched to gold by the early sun, the brooding mists under the banks at some distance down the stream, the fort, the soldiers, the piece of drift—all had distracted him . . .

He unclosed his eyes and saw again the water below him. "If I could free my hands," he thought, "I might throw off the noose and spring into the stream. By diving I could evade the bullets and, swimming vigorously, reach the bank, take to the woods and get away home. My home, thank God, is as yet outside their lines; my wife and little ones are still beyond the invader's farthest advance."

As these thoughts were flashed into the doomed man's brain . . . the captain nodded to the sergeant. The sergeant stepped aside.

II

Peyton Farquhar was a well-to-do planter, of an old and highly respected Alabama family. Being a slave owner he was naturally an original secessionist[3] and ardently devoted to the Southern cause.

One evening while Farquhar and his wife were sitting on a rustic bench near the entrance to his grounds, a gray-clad[4] soldier rode up to the gate and asked for a drink of water. Mrs. Farquhar was only too happy to serve him with her own white hands. While she was fetching the water her husband approached the dusty horseman and inquired eagerly for news from the front.

"The Yanks[5] are repairing the railroads," said the man, "and are getting ready for another advance. They have reached Owl Creek bridge, put it in order and built a stockade on the north bank. The commandant has issued an order, which is posted everywhere, declaring that any civilian caught interfering with the railroad, its bridges, tunnels or trains will be summarily hanged. I saw the order."

"How far is it to the Owl Creek bridge?" Farquhar asked.

"About thirty miles."

"Is there no force on this side the creek?"

"Only a picket post half a mile out, on the railroad, and a single sentinel at this end of the bridge."

Definitions and Clues

brooding: Hovering over or sitting still, making few movements.

noose: A loop formed by tying a knot in a rope.

evade.   Escape or avoid (*e-* means away; *-vade* refers to going). "By diving" is a clue.

planter: In this case, one who grows cotton on a large farm known in the southern United States as a plantation.

ardently: With strong commitment.

rustic: Such as might be found in the country; simple, unsophisticated (*rus-* refers to country).

stockade: An area fenced in for protection.

commandant: A commanding officer in the military.

summarily: To perform with speed and little ceremony.

picket post: A station at which one or more soldiers remain to give warning if an enemy approaches.

"Suppose a man—a civilian and student of hanging—should elude the picket post and perhaps get the better of the sentinel," said Farquhar, smiling, "what could he accomplish?"

The soldier reflected. "I was there a month ago," he replied. "I observed that the flood of last winter had lodged a great quantity of driftwood against the wooden pier at this end of the bridge. It is now dry and would burn like tow."

The lady had now brought the water, which the soldier drank. He thanked her ceremoniously, bowed to her husband and rode away. An hour later, after nightfall, he repassed the plantation, going northward in the direction from which he had come. He was a Federal scout.

III

As Peyton Farquhar fell straight downward through the bridge he lost consciousness and was as one already dead. From this state he was awakened—ages later, it seemed to him—by the pain of a sharp pressure upon his throat, followed by a sense of suffocation. . . .

Then all at once, with terrible suddenness, the light about him shot upward with the noise of a loud plash; a frightful roaring was in his ears, and all was cold and dark. The power of thought was restored; he knew that the rope had broken and he had fallen into the stream. . . .

He was not conscious of an effort, but a sharp pain in his wrist appraised him that he was trying to free his hands. He gave the struggle his attention. . . . What splendid effort!—what magnificent, what superhuman strength! Ah, that was a fine endeavor! Bravo! The cord fell away; his arms parted and floated upward, the hands dimly seen on each side in the growing light. He watched them with a new interest as first one and then the other pounced upon the noose at his neck. They tore it away and thrust it fiercely aside, its undulations resembling those of a water snake . . . He looked at the forest on the bank of the stream, saw the individual trees, the leaves and the veining of each leaf—saw the very insects upon them: the locusts, the brilliant-bodied flies, the gray spiders stretching their webs from twig to twig. He noted the prismatic colors in all the dewdrops upon a million blades of grass. The humming of the gnats that danced above the eddies of the stream, the beating of the dragonflies' wings, the strokes of the waterspiders' legs, like oars which had lifted their boat—all these made audible music. A fish slid along beneath his eyes and he heard the rush of its body parting the water.

Definitions and Clues

elude: Escape (*e-* means away).

pier: A wooden platform extending over the water.

tow: Broken fibers prepared for spinning into cloth.

appraised: Sized up or evaluated.

undulations: Movements using wavelike motions.

locusts: A kind of grasshopper.

prismatic: Like a prism, which separates white light into individual colors such as those in a rainbow.

gnats: Small flying insects that often bite.

eddies: Currents of water (or air) moving in a direction opposite to that of the main current.

audible: Capable of being heard (*aud-* refers to hearing). The first part of the sentence offers clues.

He had come to the surface facing down the stream; in a moment the visible world seemed to wheel slowly round, himself the pivotal point, and he saw the bridge, the fort, the soldiers upon the bridge . . . How coldly and pitilessly . . . fell those cruel words: "Attention, company! . . . Shoulder arms! . . . Ready! . . . Aim! . . . Fire!"

Farquhar dived—dived as deeply as he could. The water roared in his ears, yet he heard the dulled thunder of the volley and, rising again toward the surface, met shining bits of metal, singularly flattened, oscillating slowly downward. Some of them touched him on the face and hands, then fell away, continuing their descent. One lodged between his collar and neck; it was uncomfortably warm and he snatched it out.

As he rose to the surface, gasping for breath, he saw that he had been a long time under water; he was perceptibly farther downstream—nearer to safety. . . .

Suddenly he felt himself whirled round and round—spinning like a top. The water, the banks, the forests, the now distant bridge, fort and men—all were commingled and blurred. Objects were represented by their colors only; circular horizontal streaks of color—that was all he saw. In a few moments he was flung upon the gravel at the foot of the left bank of the stream—the southern bank—and behind a projecting point which concealed him from his enemies. The sudden arrest of his motion, the abrasion of one of his hands on the gravel, restored him, and he wept with delight. He dug his fingers into the sand, threw it over himself in handfuls and audibly blessed it. It looked like diamonds, rubies, emeralds; he could think of nothing beautiful which it did not resemble. The trees upon the bank were giant garden plants; he noted a definite order in their arrangement, inhaled the fragrance of their blooms. A strange, roseate light shone through the spaces among their trunks and the wind made in their branches the music of aeolian harps. He had no wish to perfect his escape—was content to remain in that enchanting spot until retaken.

A whiz and rattle of grapeshot among the branches high above his head aroused him from his dream. The baffled cannoneer had fired him a random farewell. He sprang to his feet, rushed up the sloping bank, and plunged into the forest.

All that day he traveled, laying his course by the rounding sun. The forest seemed interminable; nowhere did he discover a break in it, not even a woodman's road. He had not known that he lived in so wild a region . . .

His neck was in pain and lifting his hand to it he found it horribly swollen. He knew that it had a circle of black where the rope had bruised it. His eyes felt congested; he could no longer

---

Definitions and Clues

volley: In this case, a burst of shots.

perceptibly: Capable of being noticed ("to perceive" means to become aware of).

commingle: To mix together (*com-* refers to bringing together; mingle means to mix). The following sentence in the reading is a clue.

abrasion: A scraped area, a cut on the skin.

roseate: Rose-colored.

aeolian harps: Harps whose strings sound as the wind passes over them. Relates to Aeolis, the Greek god of winds.

grapeshot: A cluster of small iron balls shot from a cannon.

interminable: Never-ending (*in-* here means not; *-termin-* refers to an ending or boundary). The following phrase in the reading is a clue.

close them. His tongue was swollen with thirst; he relieved its fever by thrusting it forward from between his teeth into the cold air. How softly the turf had carpeted the untraveled avenue—he could no longer feel the roadway beneath his feet!

Doubtless, despite his suffering, he had fallen asleep while walking, for now he sees another scene—perhaps he has merely recovered from a delirium. He stands at the gate of his own home. All is as he left it, and all bright and beautiful in the morning sunshine. He must have traveled the entire night. As he pushes upon the gate and passes up the wide white walk, he sees a flutter of female garments; his wife, looking fresh and cool and sweet, steps down the veranda to meet him. At the bottom of the steps she stands waiting, with a smile of ineffable joy, an attitude of matchless grace and dignity. Ah, how beautiful she is! He springs forward with extended arms. As he is about to clasp her he feels a stunning blow upon the back of the neck; a blinding white light blazes all about him with a sound like the shock of a cannon—then all is darkness and silence!

Peyton Farquhar was dead; his body, with a broken neck, swung gently from side to side beneath the timbers of the Owl Creek bridge.

Definitions and Clues

turf: Grass.

delirium: The state of being confused.

veranda: A porch.

ineffable: Indescribable (*in-* here means not; *-effable* means capable of being expressed in words).

Understanding Intended Meaning

Discuss the following questions with your class.

1.   What appears to be happening to Peyton Farquhar, the man whose situation is described at the beginning of the story?

2.   For what reason do you think he is in this situation?

3.   Upon what evidence from the story do you base your conclusion?

4.   What experiences does he have during his imagined escape?

5.   What treasures in life became of the utmost importance to Farquhar in his last moments of life?

6.   Were you surprised at the ending? Explain.

Relating the Story to Your Own Life

Discuss the following questions with a classmate.

1.   Do you think Farquhar was betrayed? Explain.

2.   Have you ever felt betrayed? What was your reaction? How can such feelings be handled in a positive way?

3.   Is there any cause for which you would be willing to risk your life as did Farquhar? Explain.

4.   Have you or someone close to you been in a near-death situation? Try to recall the feelings and sensations as they happened to you or as they were described to you. Did they resemble those of Farquhar before his death?

Appreciating Descriptive Language

1.   You learned in Unit 3 that a metaphor is a comparison between two seemingly unlike things (see page 25). Personification is a kind of metaphor in that objects or ideas are compared to humans; they are given human characteristics. The author of this story makes use of personification to a great extent. For example, he speaks of a " . . . stream *racing* madly beneath his feet . . . " and "a piece of *dancing* driftwood." Find at least *four* other examples of personification from the story and list them below. In each case, underline the word or phrase that compares the object to a human.

a. _____

b. _____

c. _____

d. _____

2.   Most authors use specific actions and carefully chosen words and phrases to control the mood or the feeling of their stories. Often there are changes in mood. For example, in this story the author first establishes a feeling of foreboding. The reader senses that a terrible thing is about to happen. This foreboding then gives way to hope. Fear sits just below the surface and increases dramatically from time to time, adding great suspense. In the boxes below, list some of the actions and descriptive words and phrases that the author uses to create the moods listed.

Mood	Actions	Descriptive Words/ Phrases
Foreboding		
Hope		
Fear		

Determining Point of View

A story is usually told from the point of view of the author, or one of the characters, or some omniscient (all-knowing) being. From whose point of view is this story told? Does the point of view change? Discuss your answers with your teacher and the class.

Developing a Story Grammar

A story grammar such as the one below allows the reader to see graphically the parts of a story and how they relate to one another. Complete the story grammar, filling in the missing sections. Before you begin, consider a few definitions which may help you with the task. The *theme* is the main idea of the story. A *protagonist* is the main character or group of characters who desire something (the *main goal*). The *antagonist,* on the other hand, is usually another character or group of characters who, either directly or indirectly, prevent the protagonist from reaching the main goal. The antagonist does not necessarily have to be other characters, however. It can be nature, society, or a flaw within the protagonist. The *plot* is the series of events or happenings in the story.

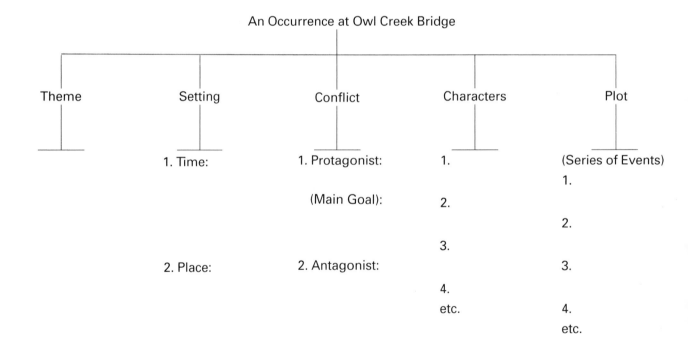

An Occurrence at Owl Creek Bridge

Theme	Setting	Conflict	Characters	Plot
	1. Time:	1. Protagonist:	1.	(Series of Events) 1.
		(Main Goal):	2.	2.
			3.	
	2. Place:	2. Antagonist:	4. etc.	3.
				4. etc.

Ideas for Discussion and/or Writing

1. Pretend you are Farquhar standing on the bridge. What might your thoughts be? Create a monologue in which you state your thoughts aloud. As an alternative you might create a dialogue with one of your executioners. Get together with one of your classmates to act out the scene.

2. In the library find out as much as you can about the American Civil War (1861–1865). Have there been similar wars fought in the country with which you are most familiar? Compare them. Consider what caused each war, the people who fought, the overall results of each war, and the war's effects on the lives of families and individuals.

3. Being executed for a crime one has committed is called capital punishment. In the library find some pros (arguments for) and cons (arguments against) of capital punishment. Consider possible alternatives. Write down the sources of your information. You may want to participate in a debate or a discussion of capital punishment.

4. Read several other stories on themes of interest to you. Your teacher may be able to help you select them. Using the model on page 68, develop a story grammar for each.

5. Would you like to try writing your own short story? If so, you will need to consider such things as point of view, descriptive language (including personification and other metaphors), and mood development. You and your classmates may want to put together a collection of your stories to share with others.

Notes

1. "An Occurrence at Owl Creek Bridge" is an excerpt from a story by Ambrose Bierce. Ambrose Bierce was an American author (1842–1914?) who served in the Union army during the Civil War. Later he became a journalist and a Washington correspondent. In 1913, feeling depressed and disillusioned, he left the country and was never seen again.

2. The Federal army was another name for the Union army.

3. A secessionist was a person who wanted the Confederacy to withdraw from the Federal Union.

4. Gray was the color of the uniforms worn by the Confederate army.

5. A Yank is another name for a person from a northern state.

Unit 8 / Anthropology

ECONOMIC RESOURCES, POWER, AND PRESTIGE

In egalitarian societies all persons have equal access to status positions and economic resources. Among the members of a !Kung band, for example, there is no visible difference in prestige, power, or wealth. Although the second man from the right holds the position of headman, he has no power, nor does he enjoy any other advantages.

In Unit 1 you learned about human behavior from a sociological perspective. You were asked to think about this perspective in relation to biological and psychological perspectives. In this unit you will learn about yet another perspective: *anthropological.* What do you think this point of view includes? Note that *anthro* means man.

Sometimes one group or individual tries to discriminate against another or treat another unfairly. Have you ever felt discriminated against? If so, how did it make you feel? Describe the situation. Why do you think you were being treated unfairly? Is it possible that those discriminating against you were afraid of you in some way?

Read the following statements. Check the ones you think are true.

a. In a society in which open social classes exist, most people stay in the class into which they were born.

b. In a society such as that of the United States, most people have the same advantages regardless of their social group.

c. Anthropologists believe that societies in which most members have the same advantages are a relatively recent development in human history.

Using Highlighting as a Study Aid

Highlighting, like marginal glossing, is a useful study aid. It can help you prepare for exams and for study in general. Notice that in the first two paragraphs of the reading selection, the major ideas are highlighted. Continue to highlight the major ideas in the remainder of the reading selection. Compare your highlighting to that of a classmate.

Societies may claim that all their citizens are equal. However, this does not usually mean that each citizen is treated the same. Differences in treatment often depend upon the social group to which one belongs, on one's age, and on one's ability. Even sex differences bring a distinction in treatment in most societies. Read to find out more about equality and what it means in different societies around the world.

Economic Resources, Power, and Prestige

CAROL R. EMBER
AND MELVIN EMBER

VARIATION IN DEGREE OF SOCIAL INEQUALITY

Some societies have customs or rules that give certain social groups greater access to economic resources, power, and prestige. Power is the ability, based on the threat of force, to make others do things they may not want to do; power is influence based on the threat of force. Prestige is respect or honor.

Anthropologists conventionally distinguish three types of societies in terms of degree of social inequality: egalitarian, rank, and class societies. Egalitarian societies have no special groups with greater access to economic resources, power, or prestige. Rank societies do not have unequal access to economic resources or to power, but they do have social groups with unequal access to prestige. Rank societies, then, are partially stratified. Class societies have unequal access to all three advantages—economic resources, power, and prestige. Table 1 summarizes these three types of societies.

Egalitarian Societies

Egalitarian societies can be found not only among hunter-gatherers, but among horticulturalists and pastoralists as well. An important point to keep in mind is that *egalitarian* does not mean that all people within such societies are the *same*. There will always be differences among individuals in age and sex and in such abilities or traits as hunting skill, perception, health, creativity, physical prowess, attractiveness, and intelligence. According to Morton Fried, *egalitarian* means that within a given society, "there are as many positions of prestige in any given age-sex grade as there are persons capable of filling them."[1] For instance, if a person can achieve status (a position of prestige) by fashioning fine spears, and

---

Definitions and Clues

stratified: Grouped into levels (*strati-* refers to horizontal layers).

horticulturalists: People who grow plants (*horti-* refers to a garden; *-cult-* refers to preparing the soil for growing plants).

pastoralists: In this case, people who herd and/or raise animals (*pastor-* refers to shepherd).

prowess: Great skill (*prow-* refers to being proud).

fashioning: Shaping something a certain way.

Table 1. Stratification in Three Types of Societies

Type of society	Some social groups have greater access to:		
	Economic resources	Power	Prestige
Egalitarian	No	No	No
Rank	No	No	Yes
Class/caste	Yes	Yes	Yes

every person in the society fashions such spears, then every person acquires status as a spear maker . . .

Any differences in prestige that do exist are not related to economic differences. Egalitarian groups depend heavily on *sharing,* which ensures equal access to economic resources despite differences in acquired prestige . . .

Just as egalitarian societies do not have social groups with unequal access to economic resources, they also do not have social groups with unequal access to power.

The Mbuti Pygmies of central Africa provide an example of a society almost totally equal: "Neither in ritual, hunting, kinship nor band relations do they exhibit any discernible inequalities of rank or advantage."[2] Their hunting bands have no leaders; recognition of the achievement of one person is not accompanied by privilege of any sort. Economic resources such as food are communally shared,

and even tools and weapons are frequently passed from person to person. Only within the family are rights and privileges differentiated.

Rank Societies

Societies with social *ranking* generally practice agriculture or herding, but not all agricultural or pastoral societies are ranked. Ranking is characterized by social groups with unequal access to prestige or status, but not unequal access to economic resources or power. Unequal access to prestige is often reflected in the position of chief, a rank to which only some members of a specified group in the society can succeed.

In rank societies, the position of chief is at least partially hereditary. The criterion of superior rank in some Polynesian societies, for example, was genealogical. Usually the eldest

---

Definitions and Clues

kinship: Relating to one's family.

band: Here it means a group of people united for a common purpose.

discernible: That which can be seen or detected.

communally: Related to a community (*commun-* refers to having things in common).

criterion: A standard or rule upon which a decision or judgment is made (*criter-* refers to judging). The plural form is criteria.

genealogical: Related to genealogy, the study of a family's history. A record is made of who was born to whom (*gene-* means to give birth).

son succeeded to the position of chief, and different kinship groups were differentially ranked according to their genealogical distance from the chiefly line . . .

The chief in rank society has influence but no power. He does not possess greater access to economic resources, nor is he generally excused from labor. He maintains his position and prestige by his generosity. According to our societal values, the chief may appear impoverished; but by the standards of his society, he has high status because he gives wealth away rather than keeping it.

An example of a rank society is the Swazi of South Africa. Hilda Kuper reports that the Swazi are a horticultural people who invest their chief with "ownership" of the land.[3] . . .

Among the Swazi, the chief is recognized as the lineal descendant of the first ruler of the tribe. He is selected according to the rank of his mother. Both the chief and his mother are treated with great deference, are addressed with extravagant titles, and wear elaborate regalia. Members of the chief's lineage are called the Children of the Sun, and constitute a distinct social elite. Other members of the society are ranked according to their relationship to the chief.

All Swazis, however, regardless of rank, do the same kinds of work, live in the same kinds of houses, and eat the same foods. The superior rank of the chief is evident by the many cows in his possession and by his right to organize work parties. Sharing is the principal way goods are distributed, and the chief shares (or redistributes) more than others. A man who accumulates too many cattle is in danger of public retaliation unless he shares them or lets others use them.

Respect for chiefs is often demonstrated ceremonially, as in this presentation of a special drink to a chief in the South Pacific islands of Fiji. But chiefs in rank societies do not usually have greater wealth or power.

Class Societies

In class societies, as in rank societies, there is unequal access to prestige. But unlike rank societies class societies are characterized by unequal access to economic resources and power. That is, not every person of the same sex or age has the same chance to obtain land, animals, money, or other economic benefits, or the same opportunity to exercise power.

But however social stratification came into existence (a topic we will discuss later in the reading), it has become predominant in the world only in the last few hundred years. Fully stratified societies range from somewhat open to more or less closed class or *caste systems*.

Definitions and Clues

impoverished: Very poor (*im-* here means causing to be; *-pover-* refers to poor). See previous two sentences in the reading selection.

lineal: Forming a line.

deference: Giving in to the ideas of another (*de-* means away; *-fer-* refers to carrying).

regalia: Symbols of royalty ("regal" means royal).

Open Class Systems

A class is a category of persons who have about the same opportunity to obtain economic resources and prestige. During the last fifty years, study after study has been made of classes in American towns. Sociologists have produced profiles of typical American communities, known variously as Yankee City, Middletown, Jonesville, and Old City, all of which support the premise that the United States has distinguishable, though somewhat open, social classes. Both Lloyd Warner and Paul Lunt's Yankee City study[4] and Robert and Helen Lynd's Middletown study[5] concluded that the social status or prestige of a family generally correlated with the occupation and wealth of the head of the family.

Table 2.   American Social Classes in Yankee City

Percentage of income	Percentage of population	Social classes and characteristic traits	
45% for top 20% of the population	1.4%	Upper upper:	"old family"; usually possessing wealth, but sometimes poor; active in charities. Episcopal or Congregational church, exclusive clubs.
	1.6	Lower upper:	newly rich; imitate the U-U class and long to marry into that class.
	10.2	Upper middle:	professional men or storeowners; active in civic affairs; respectable; long to be accepted by the groups above them, but almost never are.
	28.1	Lower middle:	white collar workers; respectable homeowners, schoolteachers; looked down upon by all above them. Some members of recently integrated groups, such as Irish, Italians, French-Canadians, are in this group.
	32.6	Upper lower:	"poor but honest workers"; most of their income spent on food and rent.
5% for bottom 20% of the population	25.2	Lower lower:	thought by other classes to be lazy, shiftless, sexually proficient, and promiscuous. In reality, they are simply poor.

Reprinted by permission of Yale University Press from *The Social Life of a Modern Community* by W. Lloyd Warner and Paul S. Lunt. Copyright © by Yale University Press, 1941.

Definitions and Clues

correlated: Related by using certain numerical procedures.

Towns in America have been described as having as few as two, and as many as eleven, social classes, but generally from four to six are recognized. In the Yankee City research, 99 percent of the city's 17,000 inhabitants were studied and classified over a period of several years. Warner and Lunt concluded that six groups emerged strongly enough to be called classes. These groups are summarized by characteristic traits in Table 2 . . .

On the whole, American society is a somewhat *open* society; that is, it is possible, through effort, to move from one class to another. A university education has been a major aid in moving upward. Lower-class persons may become "resocialized" at the university, which separates them from their parents and enables them to gradually learn the skills, speech, attitudes, and manners characteristic of the higher class they wish to join. So successful is this process that students from a lower class who move into a higher class may find themselves ashamed to take their new friends to their parents' homes.

Our identification with a social class begins quite early in life. The residence area chosen by our parents, our church, school, school curriculum, clubs, sports, college (or lack of college), marriage partner, and occupation are all influential in socializing us into a particular class.

Although some class societies have more open class systems than others, the greatest likelihood is that people will remain in the class of their birth. For example, the Japanese class system has become more open in the last hundred years. A 1960 study of the upper-class business elite showed that 8 percent came from lower-class and 31 percent from middle-class backgrounds.[6] This social mobility was achieved chiefly by successful passage through the highly competitive university sys-

tem. The Japanese class system is not completely open, however, for 61 percent of the business elite came from the relatively small upper class. The tendency to retain high class status even through changing times is clear.

Caste Systems

In a caste system an individual's position in society is *completely* ascribed, or determined, at birth. Upward mobility is prohibited either by law or by custom or both, and marriage is restricted to members of one's own caste. Thus, a caste is a *closed* class.

Questions basic to all stratified societies, and particularly to a caste society, have been posed by John Ruskin: "Which of us . . . is to do the hard and dirty work for the rest—and for what pay? Who is to do the pleasant and clean work, and for what pay?"[7] The questions have been answered in India by the maintenance of a rigidly constructed caste system—or hierarchy of statuses—whose underlying basis is economic; the system involves an intricate procedure for the exchange of goods and services[8] . . .

Each caste is traditionally associated with an occupation. For example, in a typical village the potter makes clay drinking cups and larger water vessels for the entire village population. In return, the principal landowner gives him a house site and supplies him twice yearly with grain. Some other castes owe the potter their services: the barber cuts his hair; the sweeper carries away his rubbish; the washer washes his clothes; the Brahman performs his children's weddings. . . .

Since World War II, the economic basis of the caste system in India has been undermined somewhat by the growing practice of giving cash payment for services. For instance, the son of a barber may be a teacher during

---

Definitions and Clues

ascribed: Assigned.
hierarchy: Classified according to rank.

the week, earning a cash salary, and confine his haircutting to weekends. However, he still remains in the barber caste (Nai) and must marry within that caste, thus reinforcing the social effects of the caste system. . . .

Although few areas of the world have developed a caste system like that of India, there are castelike features in some other societies. For example, there is the castelike status of blacks in the United States, which is determined partially by the ascribed characteristic of skin color. Until recently, there were laws in some states prohibiting a black from marrying a white. Even when interracial marriage does occur, children of the union are often regarded as having lower status, even though they may have blonde hair and fair skin. In the South, where treatment of blacks as a caste was most apparent, whites traditionally refused to eat with blacks or, until recently, to sit next to them at lunch counters, on buses, and in schools. Separate drinking fountains and toilets for blacks and whites reinforced the idea of ritual uncleanness. The economic advantages and gains in prestige enjoyed by whites are well documented.

Another example of a caste group in class society is the Eta of Japan. Unlike blacks in America, members of the Eta caste are physically indistinguishable from other Japanese. They are a hereditary, endogamous (in-marrying) group, comparable to India's untouchables. In the past, the Eta were a caste of about 400,000—segregated from other Japanese by place of residence, by denial of rights of citizenship, and by elaborate ritual. In recent years, the Eta have not only remained at the bottom of the hierarchy but have seen their ranks swell to between 1 and 3 million as a result of the downward mobility that accompanied the decline in the farm population. Their occupations are traditionally those of farm laborer, leatherworker, and basket weaver; their standard of living is very low.

The Emergence of Stratification

Anthropologists are not certain why social stratification developed. Nevertheless, they are reasonably sure that higher levels of stratification emerged relatively recently in human history. Archeological sites until about 7500 years ago do not show any evidence of inequality. Houses do not appear to vary much in size and content, and burials seem to be more or less the same, suggesting that their occupants were treated more or less the same in life and death. That stratification is a relatively recent development is also suggested by the fact that certain cultural features associated with stratification also developed relatively recently. For example, most societies that depend primarily upon agriculture or herding have social classes.[9] Since agriculture and herding developed within the past 10,000 years, we may assume that most hunter-gatherers in the distant past lacked social classes. Other recently developed cultural features associated with class stratification include fixed settlements, political integration beyond the community level, the use of money as a medium of exchange, and the presence of at least some full-time specialization.[10]

Gerhard Lenski suggests that the 10,000-year-old trend toward increasing inequality has recently been reversed. He argues that inequalities of power and privilege in industrial societies—measured in terms of the concentration of political power and the distribution of income—are less pronounced than inequalities in complex preindustrial societies. Technology in industrialized societies is so complex, he argues, that those in power are compelled to delegate some authority to

---

Definitions and Clues

India's untouchables: Those who are the victims of segregation.

archeological: Relating to ancient times (*archeo-* refers to ancient).

subordinates if the system is to work. In addition, a decline in the birth rate in industrialized societies, coupled with the need for skilled labor, has pushed the average wage of workers far above the subsistence level, resulting in greater equality in the distribution of income. Finally, Lenski suggests that the spread of the democratic ideology, and particularly its acceptance by elites, has significantly broadened the political power of the lower classes.[11] A study has tested and supported Lenski's hypothesis that inequality has decreased with industrialization. Nations that are highly industrialized exhibit a lower level of inequality than nations that are only somewhat industrialized.[12]

Clearly there are a number of questions about social stratification that require additional research, particularly the kinds of research that systematically test alternative answers. Why private property develops and why classes develop are questions to which we have no answers that are based firmly on empirical research. We also do not know whether class societies generally develop out of rank societies. Although many anthropologists take for granted the sequence of egalitarian to rank to class society, we have no evidence that such a sequence has occurred generally or even in particular places. . . . And, finally, we have no tests of theories that might explain the rise of those types of class society we call caste and slave societies. Future researchers may be able to test answers to some of these questions.

Definitions and Clues

subsistence: Meeting only basic survival needs.

ideology: A body of ideas basic to a way of thinking (*ideo-* refers to an idea).

hypothesis: An assumption or proposition under investigation (*hypo-* means under; *-thesis* means a proposition).

empirical: Relating to experiments (*em-* means in; *-piri-* refers to experimental).

Checking Your Prereading Reactions

Return to the statements on page 71. Look again at your reactions. Discuss whether your ideas have changed after reading "Economic Resources, Power, and Prestige."

Gaining Knowledge

Discuss the following questions with your class.

1.   In an egalitarian society, are all persons the same? Explain.

2.   What is the role of the chief in a rank society? In what way(s) does this person have greater privileges than the others in the group?

3.   How does an open class system differ from a caste or closed class system?

4.   How would you describe the caste system in India? Is it changing? If so, to what extent according to the reading?

5. Have open class societies been known to have castelike groups within them? Give one example from the reading of such a group and tell how it is like a caste.

6. What do anthropologists think they know about the development of social stratification? What questions remain unanswered?

7. According to Gerhard Lenski, what factors have contributed to a reversal in the trend toward social stratification?

Using Highlighting to Write a Summary

Reread the portions of the text that you highlighted. Use them to write a brief summary of the reading. Compare your summary with that of a classmate and make any changes that seem appropriate.

Making Inferences

Discuss the following questions with your class.

1. According to the Yankee City and the Middletown studies, what main factors appear to be related to prestige in an open class society? Why do you think this might be true?

2. What seems to be the best way to move to a higher class in an open class society?

Looking at a Table Critically

Look at Table 2 on page 75. Notice that it was first printed in 1941. Using your own knowledge of social classes in the United States or current information you find in the library, answer these questions and discuss them with your class.

1. Do the same social classes exist today?

2. If so, are the characteristic traits still appropriate? Modify any that you feel need to be changed.

Relating to Culture

Describe the culture with which you are most familiar. Consider the access to economic resources, power, and prestige. Discuss your ideas with a small group.

Ideas for Discussion and/or Writing

1. Describe what you think would be the ideal society in terms of access to economic resources, power, and prestige. Your description may take one of several forms: an essay, an article for a periodical, or a short story. Discuss your plans with your teacher and at least one classmate before you begin.

2.   In your opinion, by what nonviolent means can groups and individuals achieve more equality within a given society or institution? Consider one or more of the following groups. Make your arguments as specific as possible.

▶ an ethnic minority group

▶ women

▶ a religious minority group

▶ the poor

▶ a political minority group

▶ the disabled

▶ other groups

3.   As a long-term project, choose two or more novels, plays, biographies, and/or auto-biographies about groups or individuals in conflict over rights to equal access to economic resources, power, or prestige. Compare their situations in as many ways as you can. Several readings are suggested below.

Children of a Lesser God (play) by Mark Medoff
   A deaf girl struggles to be a part of the society from which she feels alienated.

The Diary of a Young Girl (autobiography) by Anne Frank
   Anne Frank, a Jewish girl, records her experiences while hiding in Amsterdam from the Nazis.

Eleanor and Franklin (biography) by Joseph P. Lash
   Focuses on the courageous wife of an American President as she champions rights for women and other disadvantaged groups.

The Grapes of Wrath (novel) by John Steinbeck
   Agricultural laborers try to survive during the dark years of the Depression in the United States.

Laughing Boy (novel) Oliver La Farge
   A young Native American boy's existence is vividly portrayed.

The Milagro Beanfield War (novel) by John Nichols
   Hispanic and Native American landowners in New Mexico attempt to protect their way of life from money-hungry developers.

Of Mice and Men (novel and play) by John Steinbeck
   A couple of itinerant ranch hands dream of a better life but become caught up in a tragedy.

Oliver Twist (novel) by Charles Dickens
   The experiences of a poor young boy recruited into a life of petty crime.

To Kill a Mockingbird (novel) by Harper Lee
   Portrays an attempt to gain justice for a black man on trial in the south.

View from the Bridge (play) by Arthur Miller
   The struggle of dock workers drawn into a violent existence.

Notes

1.   Morton H. Fried, *The Evolution of Political Society* (New York: Random House, 1967), p. 33.

2.   Michael G. Smith, "Pre-Industrial Stratification Systems," in Neil J. Smelser and Seymour Martin Lipset, eds., *Social Structure and Mobility in Economic Development* (Chicago: Aldine, 1966), p. 152.

3.   Hilda Kuper, *A South African Kingdom: The Swazi* (New York: Holt, Rinehart and Winston, 1963).

4.   W. Lloyd Warner and Paul S. Lunt, *The Social Life of a Modern Community* (New Haven: Yale University Press, 1941).

5.   Robert S. Lynd and Helen Merrell Lynd, *Middletown* (New York: Harcourt, Brace, 1929); idem, *Middletown in Transition* (New York: Harcourt, Brace, 1937).

6.   Edward Norbeck, "Continuities in Japanese Social Stratification," in Leonard Plotnicov and Arthur Tuden, eds., *Essays in Comparative Social Stratification* (Pittsburgh: University of Pittsburgh Press, 1970).

7.   John Ruskin, "Of Kings' Treasures," in John D. Rosenberg, ed., *The Genius of John Ruskin: Selections from His Writings* (New York: Braziller, 1963), pp. 296–314.

8.   See Oscar Lewis, with the assistance of Victor Barnouw, *Village Life in Northern India* (Urbana: University of Ilinois Press, 1958).

9.   Data from Robert B. Textor, comp., *A Cross-Cultural Summary* (New Haven: HRAF Press, 1967).

10.   Ibid.

11.   Gerhard Lenski, *Power and Privilege* (New York: McGraw-Hill, 1966), pp. 308–318.

12.   Phillips Cutright, "Inequality: A Cross-National Analysis," *American Sociological Review* 32 (1967): 564.

Unit 9 / Mathematics
NUMERAL SYSTEMS

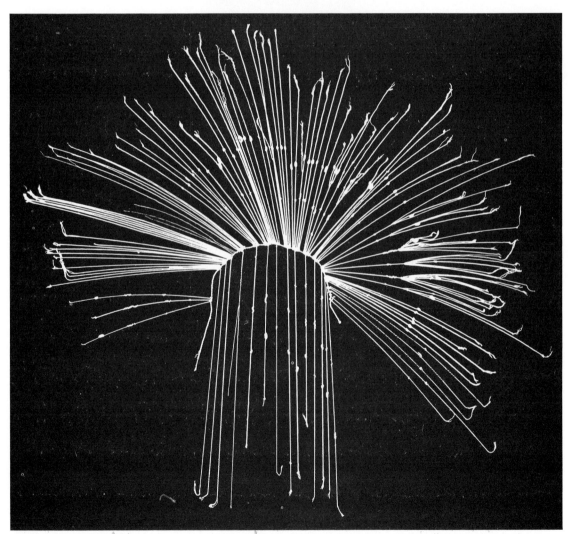

Woven llama-wool quipu. This string represents an astronomical record; each string and knot has a definite (and varying) significance.

Humankind has always possessed the ability to invent systems that meet specific needs. Numeral systems are further evidence of this ability. For what reasons do you think humans created numeral systems? In what dramatic ways would our lives be different had we not created such systems?

Do you have any ideas about *how* numeral systems may have evolved from the very simple to the more complex? Based on your current knowledge, try to form some hypotheses about what the process may have been.

Read the following statements. Check the ones you think are true.

a. Animals have been known to show an ability for counting.

b. No single numbering system during ancient times was widely used at the international level.

c. Most numbering systems do not have a "base" number from which other numbers are determined.

d. All numbering systems evolved in pretty much the same way.

Using Highlighting as a Study Aid

Highlighting the major ideas can be a useful study aid. As you learned in Unit 8, such a procedure can help prepare for exams and for study in general. Highlight what you feel to be the main ideas in the reading selection. Compare your highlighting with that of a classmate.

Many different counting systems have been used by different peoples. Although there appear to be vast differences among them because the symbols used are so diverse, further analysis reveals that they are really very similar. Read to find out just how similar some of these systems really are and some interesting speculations on how they may have developed.

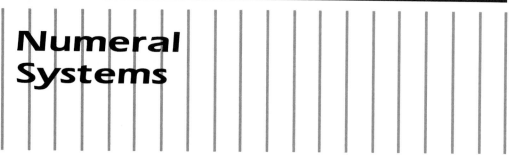

Numeral Systems

HOWARD EVES

PRIMITIVE COUNTING

The concept of *number* and the process of *counting* developed so long before the time of recorded history that the manner of this development is largely conjectural. It is not difficult, though, to imagine how it probably came about. It seems fair to argue that humans, even in most primitive times, had some number sense, at least to the extent of recognizing *more* and *less* when some objects were added to or taken from a small group, for studies have shown that some animals possess such a sense. With the gradual evolution of society, simple counting became imperative. A tribe had to know how many members it had and how many enemies, and a man found it necessary to know if his flock of sheep was decreasing in size. Probably the earliest way of keeping a count was by some simple tally method, employing the principle of one-to-one correspondence. In keeping a count on sheep, for example, one finger per sheep could be turned under. Counts could also be maintained by making collections of pebbles or sticks, by making scratches in the dirt or on a stone, by cutting notches in a piece of wood, or by tying knots in a string. Then, perhaps later, an assortment of vocal sounds was developed as a word tally against the number of objects in a small group. And still later, with the refinement of writing, an assortment of symbols was devised to stand for these numbers. Such an imagined development is supported by reports of anthropologists in their studies of present-day primitive peoples.

In the earlier stages of the period of vocal counting, different sounds (words) were used, for example, for *two* sheep and *two* men. (Consider, for example, in English: *team* of horses, *span* of mules, *yoke* of oxen, *brace* of partridge, *pair* of shoes, *couple* of days.) The abstraction of the common property of *two,* represented by some sound considered independently of any concrete association, probably was a long time in arriving. Our present number words in all

Definitions and Clues

conjectural: Related to conjecture, which means to guess (*con-* means together; *-ject-* refers to throwing).

likelihood originally referred to sets of certain concrete objects, but these associations, except for that perhaps relating five and hand, are now lost to us.

NUMBER BASES

When it became necessary to make more extensive counts, the counting process had to be systematized. This was done by arranging the numbers into convenient basic groups, the size of the groups being largely determined by the matching process employed. Essentially, the method was like this. Some number b was selected as a base (also called **radix** or **scale**) for counting, and names were assigned to the numbers 1, 2, . . . , b. Names for numbers larger than b were then given by combinations of the number names already selected.

Since fingers furnished such a convenient matching device, it is not surprising that 10 was ultimately chosen far more often than not for the number base b. Consider, for example, our present number words, which are formed on 10 as a base. We have the special names *one, two, . . . , ten* for the numbers 1, 2, . . . , 10. When we came to 11 we say *eleven,* which, the philologists tell us, derives from *ein lifon,* meaning "one left over," or one over ten. Similarly, *twelve* is from *twe lif* ("two over ten"). Then we have *thirteen* ("three and ten"), *fourteen* ("four and ten"), up through *nineteen* ("nine and ten"). Then comes *twenty* (*twe-tig,* or "two tens"), *twenty-one* ("two tens and one"), and so on. The word *hundred,* we are told, comes originally from a term meaning "ten times" (ten).

There is evidence that 2, 3, and 4 have served as primitive number bases. For example, there are natives of Queensland who count "one, two, two and one, two twos, much," and some African pygmies count "a, oa, ua, oa-oa, oa-oa-a, and oa-oa-oa" for 1, 2, 3, 4, 5, and 6. A certain tribe of Tierra del Fuego has its first few number names based on 3, and some South American tribes similarly use 4.

As might be expected, the **quinary scale,** or number system based on 5, was the first scale to be used extensively. To this day some South American tribes count by hands: "one, two, three, four, hand, hand and one," and so on. The Yukaghirs of Siberia use a mixed scale by counting "one, two, three, three and one, five, two threes, one more, two fours, ten with one missing, ten." German peasant calendars used a quinary scale as late as 1800.

There is also evidence that 12 may have been used as a base in prehistoric times, chiefly in relation to measurements. Such a base may have been suggested by the approximate number of lunations in a year, or perhaps because 12 has so many integral fractional parts. At any rate, we have 12 as the number of inches in a foot, ounces in the ancient pound, pence in a shilling, lines in an inch, hours about the clock, months in a year, and the words *dozen* and *gross* are used as higher units.

The **vigesimal scale,** or number system based on 20, has been widely used, and recalls man's barefoot days. This scale was used by American Indian peoples, and is best known in the well-developed Mayan number system. Celtic traces of a base 20 are found in French, Gaelic, Danish, and Welsh. The Greenlanders use "one man" for 20, "two men" for 40, and so on. In English we have the frequently used word *score.*

Definitions and Clues

lunations: Lapses of time (approximately 30 days) between two successive moons (*luna-* means moon).

The **sexagesimal scale,** or number system based on 60, was used by the ancient Babylonians, and is still used when measuring time and angles in minutes and seconds.

WRITTEN NUMBER SYSTEMS

In addition to spoken numbers, finger numbers were at one time widely used. Indeed, the expression of numbers by various positions of the fingers and hands probably predates the use of either number symbols or number names. Thus, the early written symbols for 1, 2, 3, and 4 were invariably the suitable number of vertical or horizontal strokes, representing the corresponding number of raised or extended fingers, and the word *digit* (that is, "finger") for the number 1 through 9 can be traced to the same source.

In time, finger numbers were extended to include the largest numbers occurring in commercial transactions, and by the Middle Ages they had become international. In the ultimate development, the numbers 1, 2, . . . , 9 and 10, 20, . . . , 90 were represented on the left hand, and the numbers 100, 200, . . . , 900 and 1000, 2000, . . . , 9000 on the right hand. In this way, any number up to 10,000 was representable by the use of the two hands. Pictures of the finger numbers were given in later arithmetic books. For example, using the left hand, 1 was represented by partially folding down the little finger, 2 by partially folding down the little and ring fingers, 3 by partially holding down the little, ring, and middle fingers, 4 by folding down the middle and ring fingers, 5 by folding down the middle finger, 6 by folding down the ring finger, 7 by completely folding down the little finger, 8 by completely folding down the little and ring fingers, and 9 by completely folding down the little, ring, and middle fingers.

Finger numbers had the advantage of transcending language differences, but, like the vocal numbers, lacked permanence and were not suitable for performing calculations. We have already mentioned the use of marks and notches as early ways of recording numbers. In such devices we probably have the first attempt at writing. At any rate, various written number systems gradually evolved from these primitive efforts to make permanent number records. A written number is called a numeral, and we now turn our attention to a simple classification of early numeral systems.

SIMPLE GROUPING SYSTEMS

Perhaps about the earliest type of numeral system that was developed is that which has been called a simple grouping system. In such a system some number b is selected for number base and symbols are adopted for 1, b, b^2, b^3, and so on. Then any number is expressed by using these symbols *additively,* each symbol being repeated the required number of times. The following illustrations will clarify the underlying principle.

A very early example of a simple grouping system is that furnished by the Egyptian hieroglyphics, employed as far back as 3400 B.C. and chiefly used by the Egyptians when making inscriptions on stone. Although the hieroglyphics were sometimes used on other writing media than stone, the Egyptians early developed two considerably more rapid writing forms for work

---

Definitions and Clues

hieroglyphics: The ancient Egyptian writing system in which pictures are used to represent words or sounds (*-glyph-* refers to carving).

on papyrus, wood, and pottery. The earlier of these forms was a running script, known as the hieratic, derived from the hieroglyphic and used by the priesthood. From the hieratic there later evolved the demotic writing, which was adopted for general use. The hieratic and demotic numeral systems are not of the simple grouping type.

The Egyptian hieroglyphic numeral system is based on the scale of 10. The symbols adopted for 1 and the first few powers of 10 are

1 | a vertical staff, or stroke

10   ∩   a heel bone, or hobble, or yoke

10^2 ℗   a scroll, or coil of rope

10^3 🪷   a lotus flower

10^4 𝌀   a pointing finger

10^5 ⌐   a burbot fish, or tadpole

10^6 ⚉   a man in astonishment, or a god holding up the universe

Any number is now expressed by using these symbols additively, each symbol being repeated the required number of times. Thus,

$$13015 = 1(10^4) + 3(10^3) + 1(10) + 5 = \text{𝌀 🪷🪷🪷 ∩ |||||}$$

We have written this number from left to right, although it was more customary for the Egyptians to write from right to left.

The early Babylonians, lacking papyrus and having little access to suitable stone, resorted principally to clay as a writing medium. The inscription was pressed into a wet clay tablet by a stylus, the writing end of which may have been a sharp isosceles triangle. By tilting the stylus slightly from the perpendicular one could press either the vertex angle or a base angle of the isosceles triangle into the clay, producing two forms of wedge-shaped (cuneiform) characters.

Definitions and Clues

papyrus: A kind of paper used in ancient times and made from the plant *cyperus papyrus.*

isosceles: Having two equal sides.

stylus: A pointed tool used for engraving or writing.

vertex angle: The point in a triangle opposite to and farthest away from the base.

The finished tablet was then baked in an oven to a time-resisting hardness that resulted in a permanent record. On cuneiform tablets dating from 2000 B.C. to 200 B.C. numbers less than 60 are expressed by a simple grouping system to base 10, and it is interesting that the writing is often simplified by using a subtractive symbol. The subtractive symbol and the symbols for 1 and 10 are

respectively, where the symbol for 1 and the two parts making up the subtractive symbol are obtained by using the vertex angle of the isosceles triangle, and the symbol for 10 is obtained by using one of the base angles. As examples of written numbers employing these symbols, we have

$$25 = 2(10) + 5 =$$

and

$$38 = 40 - 2 =$$

MULTIPLICATIVE GROUPING SYSTEMS

There are instances where a simple grouping system developed into what may be called a multiplicative grouping system. In such a system, after a base b has been selected, symbols are adopted for $1, 2, \ldots, b - 1$, and a second set of symbols for $b, b^2, b^3, \ldots$. The symbols of the two sets are employed *multiplicatively* to show how many units of the higher groups are needed. Thus, if we should designate the first nine numbers by the usual symbols, but designate 10, 100, and 1000 by $a, b, c,$ say, then in a multiplicative grouping system we would write

$$5625 = 5c6b2a5.$$

The traditional Chinese-Japanese numeral system is a multiplicative grouping system to base 10. Writing vertically, the symbols of the two basic groups and of the number 5625 are

Example: 5625

4 四
5 五
6 六
7 七
8 八
9 九

百
二
十
五

Checking Your Prereading Reactions

Return to the statements on page 83. Look again at your reactions. Discuss whether your ideas have changed after reading "Numeral Systems."

Understanding Intended Meaning

Discuss the following questions with your class.

1. For what reasons did primitive counting processes develop?

2. Why did counting processes have to be systematized in order to make more extensive counts?

3. What number is most commonly used as a base? Explain why.

4. What other numbers have been used as a base? In what way may each have been convenient?

5. How did the word "digit" come about?

6. What was the international number system employed during the Middle Ages?

Using Highlighting to Write a Summary

Reread the portions of the text that you highlighted. Use them to write a brief summary of the reading. Compare your summary with that of a classmate and make any changes that seem appropriate.

Making Comparisons

Work with a small group to complete the following tasks.

1. Show how the simple grouping system of the Egyptians compares with that of the Babylonians. How are they alike? How are they different?

2. Compare the author's hypotheses with the ones you and your class formed before reading this selection.

Relating to Culture

Complete the following tasks with a small group of classmates who share the language with which you are most familiar.

Describe the systematized counting process of that language. What is the base? How are numbers formed from that base? Compare it with some of the other systems in the reading selection.

Applying Knowledge

1. Look up the symbols used in Roman numerals either in a dictionary or an encyclopedia. Use them to write the current year. Does the Roman system fit easily into one of the categories mentioned in the reading selection? Discuss your answer with your class.

2. With a small group of students, devise a new numbering system employing any symbols you wish. Use it to write your age, phone number, address, and identification numbers to which you may have been assigned. See if other classmates can figure them out.

Ideas for Discussion and/or Writing

1. Choose a number system about which you have a little knowledge. In the library try to find out as much as you can about how it may have developed. Demonstrate how it works to others in your class.

2. Compare the system you know best with one other system used in the world today. First find out as much about the other system as you can. You may need to do some research in the library. Then describe both systems and demonstrate their advantages and disadvantages.

3. Consider the numbering system with which you are most familiar. Do you think it will ever change? Why or why not?

Unit 10 / Psychology

RESEARCH FOUNDATIONS

By sitting behind a one-way mirror, the psychologist can observe the child at play and record his observations without influencing or interfering with the child's behavior.

The word "research" may be intimidating to some people. Knowing more about how research is conducted may remove some of the mystery often associated with it. Do you personally know of any research studies that have been done on human behavior? What were the results? Do you know how the studies were conducted?

If you could answer one question about human behavior, what would that question be? Is it a question that could be researched? If so, how might you go about it?

Read the following statements. Check the ones you think are true.

a. Observations of the drawings of children would not be considered a proper inclusion in a research study.

b. All research methods in psychology are related to the observation of behavior.

c. One of the drawbacks of the survey as a research tool is that it is so much more difficult to score than most other measures.

d. In a controlled experiment, it is important for the researcher to attempt to control any conditions that might have an effect on the conclusions.

Flagging Main Ideas

Use marginal glossing, highlighting, or a combination of the two to flag the main ideas in the reading selection (see examples on pages 41 and 72).

Many of us have read studies about what humans tend to do in certain situations. They may react to stress in a laboratory environment or respond to hypothetical questions about dating habits. However, we may not have given much thought to the means by which these studies were accomplished. Read this selection to get a bird's-eye view of the research that currently is being carried out to discover more about human behavior.

RESEARCH FOUNDATIONS

PHILIP G. ZIMBARDO

Research in science is a systematic search for information. It is based on the scientific method, which is a set of attitudes and procedures for gathering and interpreting objective information in such a way as to minimize sources of error and yield dependable generalizations. Scientific knowledge is built on a base of empirical evidence—that is, evidence obtained through the observation of perceivable events, or *phenomena,* rather than just from opinions or beliefs or statements by an authority.

Psychological research is the *how* of what is known in psychology. Basic to research in psychology, as in other sciences, are (a) keeping complete records of observations and data analysis in a format that other researchers can understand and evaluate; (b) communicating one's findings and conclusions in ways that allow independent observers to replicate (repeat) the findings; and (c) building knowledge as new findings are integrated into previous ones.

Psychology is a *behavioral* science because what is observed is either actual behavior, as when the speed of responding to a stimulus is measured, or the products of behavior, as when the drawings of children are observed. But behavior occurs in many forms and guises that often elude any ready explanation. Researchers ideally will insist on adequate supporting evidence for any conclusion while being open to the possibility that what is already "known" may turn out to be inaccurate. . . .

Definitions and Clues

stimulus: Anything that causes or is thought to cause a response. (Stimuli is the plural).

guises: (pronounced guys-es) Outward appearances (similar to disguises).

BASIC METHODS FOR GATHERING DATA

All research methods in psychology are based on observation of behavior. They range from observation of natural, ongoing behavior in unrestricted settings to observation under focused, highly controlled, artificial conditions where the researcher changes the stimulus conditions and limits the responses that are possible. The five methods often used in psychological research are naturalistic observation, surveys, interviews, tests, and controlled experiments . . .

Naturalistic Observation

Observing some naturally occurring behavior with no attempt to change or interfere with it is called naturalistic observation. For example, you might sit behind a one-way glass and observe preschoolers' play without their knowing you were there. You might simply record the ongoing behavior you noticed and considered worth recording. Or you might focus on particular factors in the situation, such as how often each child initiates an interaction with another or how often each child is chosen as a play partner. Any such factor that varies in amount of kind is called a variable. You would find that the children differ greatly regarding these variables. From your observations of each child's interaction patterns, you might make inferences about popularity or social isolation. Or you might look for other variables in the situation—for example, other behaviors or stimulus conditions that were often associated with initiating play behavior or being chosen.

Naturalistic observation can be conducted in the laboratory or in the "field," which is any setting outside the laboratory where there is ongoing, "natural" behavior to be observed . . .

Naturalistic observation is especially useful in the early stages of an investigation for discovering the extent of some phenomenon or getting an idea of what the important variables and relationships might be. The data from naturalistic observation often provide clues for the investigator to use in formulating a hypothesis to test by other research methods.

Surveys

A survey is a method of gathering information from a large number of people. Self-report information is gathered in response to a list of questions that follows a fixed format. Questioning may be done face-to-face or by mail or telephone. The information gathered is fairly superficial and easily scorable. Questions may be about the individuals' knowledge, attitudes, opinions, feelings, expectations, or behavior.

Surveys can be helpful in establishing how strong a particular reaction is among a given population of people, how widespread a problem is, or what the significant issues are from the viewpoint of the public. A summary of survey data on what types of people and situations make college students feel shy is shown in the table.

What Makes You Shy?

Situations	Percentage of Shy Students
Where I am focus of attention—large group (as when giving a speech)	73%
Of lower status	56%
Social situations in general	55%
New situations in general	55%
Requiring assertiveness	54%
Where I am being evaluated	53%
Where I am focus of attention—small group	52%
One-to-one different-sex interactions	48%
Of vulnerability (need help)	48%
Small task-oriented groups	28%
One-to-one same-sex interactions	14%
Other People	
Strangers	70%
Opposite sex	64%
Authorities by virtue of their knowledge	55%
Authorities by virtue of their role	40%
Relatives	21%
Elderly people	12%
Friends	11%
Children	10%
Parents	8%

From Philip G. Zimbardo. *Shyness: What It Is, What to Do About It.* Copyright © 1977, Addison-Wesley, Reading, Mass. Reprinted with permission.

Interviews

An interview is a face-to-face dialogue between a researcher and an individual for the purpose of obtaining detailed information about the individual. Interviews conducted for research purposes are interactive, in that the researcher varies the questioning to follow up on what the individual says; nonverbal behavior such as fidgeting, hesitation, or emotionality are also part of the data recorded. The interviewer is sensitive to the process of the interaction as well as to the information revealed.

Good interviewers are able to establish *rapport,* a positive social relationship with the interviewee that encourages trust and sharing of personal information. In some cases, data may be accumulated over many interviews.

Psychological Tests

Psychological tests are measuring instruments used to assess an individual's standing relative to others on some mental or behavioral characteristic, such as intelligence, vocational interests, values, aptitudes, or scholastic achievement. Each test consists of a set of questions, problems, or activities, the responses to which are assumed to be indicators of a particular psychological function. Where feasible, group tests permit information to be obtained quickly from large numbers of people without the cost of trained individuals to administer the tests.

Typically, test performance is used to predict how the person will probably behave in a particular later situation. For example, SAT scores are predictors of grades in college; scores on a test of mechanical ability indicate which individuals are highest in the abilities needed for mechanical work . . .

The Controlled Experiment

A controlled experiment is a research method in which observations are made of specific behavior under systematically varied conditions. The investigator manipulates one or more stimulus variables and observes the effects on one or more behaviors. Controlled experiments are used for testing hypotheses. They help determine how two or more variables are related and whether there is a cause-effect relationship between them—that is, between a particular condition and a later response.

In the simplest experiment, the form or amount of one stimulus variable is changed systematically under carefully controlled, often quite restrictive, conditions, and a response variable is observed to see if it changes, too. The stimulus that is changed and used to predict the response is called the independent variable. The response is the unit of behavior whose form or amount is expected to *depend* on the changes in the independent variable; it is called the dependent variable . . .

To determine that it is *only* the independent variable, and not other factors, that is causing the behavioral change, the experimenter attempts to control or at least account for the effect of all extraneous conditions. This can be done in three ways: through the use of experimental and control groups, random assignment, and controlled procedures.

Definitions and Clues

aptitudes: Abilities to develop certain skills or acquire knowledge (*apt-* here means quick to comprehend).

extraneous: Present but nonessential (*extra-* in this case means outward).

The subjects in an experiment are the individuals whose behavior is being observed. They are assigned to either the experimental group—the group exposed to the independent variable—or to the control group—the group exposed to all the conditions of the experiment *except* for the independent variable. Subjects are assigned to a group by a chance procedure called random assignment (similar to flipping a coin). Each subject thus has an equal chance of being in either the experimental or the control group. The purpose of random assignment is to make the different groups in the experiment as similar as possible before they are exposed to the independent variable. In this way, if behavioral differences are found between these groups, the differences can be attributed to the presence or absence of the independent variable and not to some initial difference in ability or experience, for example.

Another aspect of control in scientific experiments is the use of *controlled procedures,* procedures that attempt to hold constant all variables and conditions other than those related to the hypothesis being tested. Instructions, temperature, time allowed, how the responses are recorded, and so on need to be as similar as possible for all subjects to ensure that their experience is the same *except for* the difference in the independent variable.

An example of a controlled experiment is outlined in the *Close-up* below . . .

Although we learn about behavior from a number of sources, the cornerstone of scientific psychology is the controlled experiment. Yet it is not always possible to perform experiments to test hypotheses. Sometimes the phenomenon is too broad to be reduced to specific variables that can be manipulated (e.g., mob behavior or the effects of excessive environmental overload). Or the independent variable cannot be manipulated for practical reasons (e.g., the effects of being in love or of being divorced) or for ethical reasons (e.g., heredity in humans or reactions to extreme stress).

CLOSE-UP

Aging, Health, and a Sense of Control

It has long been assumed that the health problems that accompany growing old are genetically programmed into the species. But consider an alternate hypothesis—namely, that age-related decline in health is in part psychologically determined and not solely biological in origin . . .

Judith Rodin (1983) and her colleagues have done just that in an extended series of studies. We will cite one of her experiments to illustrate the sequence of events in a controlled experiment.

Rodin hypothesized that training which increased subjects' sense of control and reduced their feelings of lack of control would result in a variety of changes in three classes of variables: attitudes, behavior, and health status. Four months before the experimental treatment was to begin, 40 elderly female residents in a nursing home were selected and given extensive interviews covering issues related to perceived control, stress, and personal problems. In addition, behavioral observations were made, blood pressure and urine tests were given, and general ratings of health status were recorded. (None of the patients was acutely ill, and all were able to walk without assistance.)

The subjects were matched on age and length of residence and then randomly assigned to one of three groups: the experimental group, which would receive training; an "attention" control group, which would receive no training but spend the same amount of time with a psychologist just talking about problems of the elderly; and a second control group, which would receive no special attention . . .

The experimental group received two sessions of training for three weeks by psychologists who were unaware of the pretest data. The training procedure taught these elderly patients to minimize negative self-statements and use positive self-statements. They were also given training in how to be more active

contributors to their own experience and how to solve problems regarding potential health hazards. It was hypothesized that this training would affect the intervening variable, *sense of control.*

One month after the experimental period, the pretest procedures were repeated as a post-test. An estimate of stresses that had occurred naturally in the residential setting was also made. As predicted, the women in the experimental group, on the average, were better able than those in the control groups to deal with stresses in their environment and better able to modify conditions that gave rise to problems. They participated more in activities, were more happy, social, and energetic, and felt that they had more freedom to effect change and determine relevant outcomes in their environment. Levels of stress-related hormones in the urine were also significantly reduced, and their general health patterns were shown to be improved. On several of the post-test measures, the attention control group were slightly better than the no-attention control group, but the differences were not statistically significant.[1] On measures taken eighteen months later, the improvement of the experimental group had continued.

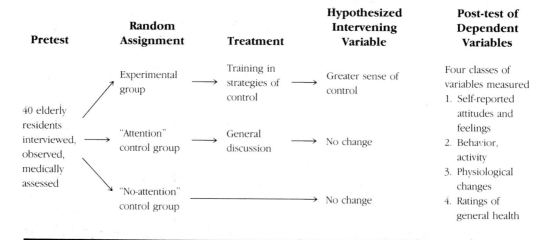

Checking Your Prereading Reactions

Return to the statements on page 92. Look again at your reactions. Discuss whether your ideas have changed after reading "Research Foundations."

Understanding Intended Meaning

Discuss the following questions with your class.

1. What is the "base" of scientific knowledge?

2. Empirical research in psychology involves three tasks. What are they?

3. Why is psychology called a *behavioral* science?

4. In what basic ways is an interview different from a survey?

5. What main advantage do psychological tests have over other methods of gathering data?

6. What is an "independent" variable? How does it differ from a "dependent" variable? Give an example of each.

7. How does a controlled experiment differ from naturalistic observation?

8. In what three ways can a researcher attempt to determine that it is only the independent variable, not other factors, that is affecting the dependent variable? Briefly explain each.

Using Study Aids to Write a Summary

Reread your marginal glossing and/or the portions of the text that you highlighted. Use them to write a brief summary of the reading. Compare your summary with that of a classmate and make any changes that seem appropriate.

Diagraming Relationships to Aid Study

By creating a diagram such as the one below, you can gain a better perspective on how ideas relate to one another. In addition, your recall is aided by seeing these relationships graphically. Find the section in the reading selection dealing with controlled experiments. Fill in the diagram with a definition, examples, and uses. Compare your diagram with those of your classmates and make any changes that seem appropriate. You may want to create diagrams for the other categories mentioned in the text.

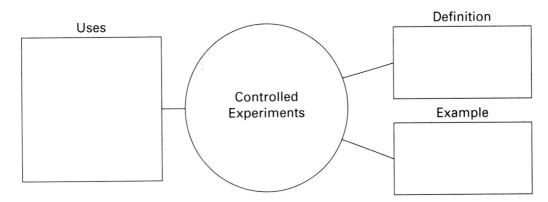

Uses — Controlled Experiments — Definition — Example

Applying Knowledge

Read the *Close-up* on pages 97–98 and discuss the following questions with a classmate.

1. What was the hypothesis being tested?
2. Who were the subjects? Briefly describe them.
3. What chief method was used to gather data in support of the hypothesis?
4. Was any pretest data collected? If so, describe it.
5. What was the independent variable?
6. What is an "hypothesized intervening variable"? Mention the one present in this study.
7. What were the dependent variables?
8. How did the researcher try to ensure that the independent variable was the only factor affecting the dependent variables?
9. What training did the subjects in the experimental group receive during the treatment?
10. What did the post-test consist of? What were the results?

Interpreting a Table and Relating It to Your Own Life

Study the table on page 95 (*What Makes You Shy?*). Discuss the following questions with a small group.

1. What method of gathering data was used?
2. In what kinds of situations did the subjects appear to be the least shy?
3. Being with what kind of people seemed to make the subjects most shy?
4. Respond to the shyness survey yourself. How do your own reactions compare to those of the subjects in the study? How do they compare to those of a classmate?

Synthesizing Knowledge

Answer the following questions. Then share your answers with your class.

1. What might be some problems with controlled experiments in gathering data for studying human behavior? Might other, perhaps more subjective, methods work better for some kinds of studies?

2. Think about the questions in the chart on the next page. Decide what kind or kinds of research might be most appropriate for answering each question (naturalistic observation, surveys, interviews, psychological tests, controlled experiments). Write the name or names of the methods. Be ready to justify your choices to your class.

Research Question	Research Method(s)
1. What portion of the population of a given country are satisfied with their jobs?	
2. Do persons receiving massive doses of vitamin C have fewer colds than those receiving no vitamin C?	
3. Do teachers tend to favor some students over others when responding to their questions?	
4. Has a specific individual's attitude toward school changed over time? If so, what factors, according to the individual, have influenced the change?	
5. What is the aptitude of a given individual for being a mechanic compared to thousands of other individuals?	

Ideas for Discussion and/or Writing

1.   From a recent psychological journal in the library, choose a research study whose results interest you. Describe the study in terms of its methods and its implications. How might you have improved the methods used if you had you been the researcher?

2.   Set up a hypothesis involving some question about human behavior. Describe how you might set up your research. What method or combination of methods might you use? What important implications might the results have? You might consider actually carrying out the research if time permits and if the study is not too complex.

3.   Create a survey to test a hypothesis you have created. Give it to your classmates as well to others on your campus. What conclusions are indicated?

4.   Use interviews to test a hypothesis you have created. Decide what questions you will ask and to whom you will ask them. Share your results with your classmates.

Notes

1.   Statistical significance refers to specific mathematical procedures used to determine the probability of the same results occurring if the study were to be repeated.

CREDITS

Readings are reprinted with the permission of the following:

A SOCIOLOGICAL PERSPECTIVE by Donald A. Hobbs and Stuart J. Blank. From *Sociology and the Human Experience,* 4th ed., by Donald A. Hobbs and Stuart J. Blank. New York: Macmillan, 1986, pp. 25–27.

CREATIVITY by Duane Preble and Sarah Preble. From *Artforms: An Introduction to Visual Arts,* 3rd ed., by Duane and Sarah Preble. New York: Harper and Row, 1985, pp. 16–26.

THE FAMOUS DEAF COMPOSER: LUDWIG VAN BEETHOVEN by Roger Kamien. From *Music: An Appreciation,* 3rd ed., by Roger Kamien. New York: McGraw-Hill, 1984, pp. 267–272.

THE IMPACT OF COMPUTERS ON PEOPLE by Donald H. Sanders. From *Computers Today,* 3rd ed., by Donald H. Sanders. New York: McGraw-Hill, 1988, pp. 126–135.

SURVIVAL IN THE WILD: THE PREDATOR AND THE PREY by Cecie Starr and Ralph Taggart. From *Biology: The Unity and Diversity of Life,* 4th ed., by Cecie Starr and Ralph Taggart. Belmont, CA: Wadsworth, 1987, pp. 676–683.

IMMIGRANTS TO THE UNITED STATES DURING THE NINETEENTH CENTURY: THE IRISH AND THE GERMANS by Robert Divine, T. H. Breen, George Fredrickson, and R. Hal Williams. From *America: Past and Present,* 2nd ed., by Robert Divine, T. H. Breen, George Fredrickson, and R. Hal Williams. Copyright © 1987, 1984 by Scott, Foresman and Company. Reprinted by permission.

AN OCCURRENCE AT OWL CREEK BRIDGE by Ambrose Bierce. From *Collected Writings of Ambrose Bierce.* Secaucus, NJ: Citadel Press, 1983. Used by permission of Lyle Stuart, Inc.

ECONOMIC RESOURCES, POWER, AND PRESTIGE by Carol R. Ember and Melvin Ember. From *Cultural Anthropology,* 4th ed., by Carol R. Ember and Melvin Ember. Englewood Cliffs, NJ: Prentice Hall, 1985, pp. 123–134.

NUMERAL SYSTEMS by Howard Eves. From *An Introduction to the History of Mathematics,* 5th ed., by Howard Eves. Philadelphia: CBS College Publishing, 1983, pp. 2–6, 8.

RESEARCH FOUNDATIONS by Philip G. Zimbardo. From *Psychology and Life*, 11th ed., by Philip G. Zimbardo. Copyright © 1985, 1979 by Scott, Foresman and Company. Reprinted by permission.

Grateful acknowledgment is given to the following for providing us with artwork or photographs:

page 2 — Longman has tried unsuccessfully to locate the copyright owners of this photograph, which appeared in Donald A. Hobbs, *Sociology and the Human Experience*, 4th ed., copyright © 1986 by Macmillan. It is therefore included without permission;

page 9 — copyright ARS N.Y./SPADEM, 1989;

pages 13 and 14 — from Duane and Sarah Preble, *Artforms: An Introduction to Visual Arts*, 3rd ed., copyright © 1985 by Harper & Row Publishers, Inc. Reprinted by permission of publisher;

page 18 — The Granger Collection, New York;

page 28 — courtesy Intergraph;

page 39 — John Dominis, LIFE Magazine 1967, copyright © Time Inc.;

page 42 — from Cecie Starr and Ralph Taggart, *Biology: The Unity and Diversity of Life*, 4th ed., © 1987 by Wadsworth, Inc. Reprinted by permission of the publisher;

page 55 — courtesy of The New-York Historical Society, New York City;

page 60 — South Caroliniana Library, University of South Carolina;

page 70 — Irven DeVore/Anthro-Photo;

page 74 — Katz/Anthro-Photo;

page 82 — photograph by Carmelo Guadagno, courtesy of the Museum of the American Indian, Heye Foundation;

page 91 — copyright © Marcia Weinstein, 1977.

NOTES

NOTES

NOTES

NOTES

NOTES

NOTES

NOTES

NOTES